THE
POWYS
JOURNAL

Volume XXIII

THE POWYS SOCIETY

President Glen Cavaliero

Chairman Timothy Hyman
Hon. Treasurer Anna Pawelko
Hon. Secretary Chris Thomas

The Powys Society is a registered charity, No 801332.

The Powys Society was founded in 1967 to 'establish the true literary status of the Powys family through promotion of the reading and discussion of their works', in particular those of John Cowper Powys (1872-1963), Theodore Francis Powys (1875-1953), and Llewelyn Powys (1884-1939).

The Society publishes a journal and three newsletters a year, and has an active publication programme. In addition it organizes an annual weekend conference, occasional meetings, exhibitions, and walks in areas associated with the Powys family.

The Society is an international one, attracting scholars and non-academics from around the world, and welcomes everyone interested in learning more about this remarkable family.

**Correspondence and membership enquiries
should be addressed to the Hon. Secretary
Chris Thomas
Flat D, 87 Ledbury Road, London W11 2AG
chris.d.thomas@hotmail.co.uk**

Visit the Powys Society Web Site:
www.powys-society.org

THE POWYS JOURNAL

Volume XXIII

2013

Editor
Charles Lock

Contributing Editor
Louise de Bruin

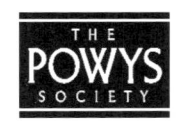

The Powys Journal is a publication of The Powys Society, appearing annually each summer. Its aim is to publish original material by members of the Powys family — notably, but not exclusively, John Cowper Powys, Theodore Francis Powys and Llewelyn Powys — and scholarly articles, book reviews and other materials relating to them, their circles and their contemporaries.

The Powys Journal is grateful to the copyright holders of the individual estates and their literary agents for their permission to print or to quote from the writings of John Cowper Powys, Theodore Francis Powys and Llewelyn Powys.

MSS **for publication and correspondence** about the contents of the *Journal* should be addressed to the Editor, Charles Lock, Professor of English Literature, University of Copenhagen, Njalsgade 130, DK-2300 Copenhagen S, Denmark; his e-mail address is:

lock@hum.ku.dk

The Powys Journal has a refereeing policy, whereby material is submitted for independent assessment. In order that the anonymity of the author and referee is preserved, articles should omit the name of the author. Please send submissions if possible by e-mail: they can be in text-only format or RTF or in Microsoft Word, but not any other word-processing programme, and should have the minimum of formatting.

Authors of printed articles will receive two copies of the *Journal*.

Orders for copies of the *Journal* should be addressed to the Society's Hon. Secretary, whose address is shown on page 2.

© 2013. Copyright is retained by the authors and, for other material, by the Editor or as otherwise stated.

Cover and title-page design: Bev Craven

Typeset in Adobe Caslon in InDesign by Jerry Bird

Publication Manager: Louise de Bruin

Printed and bound by Hobbs the Printers Ltd, Totton, Hampshire

ISSN 0962-7057

ISBN 978-1-874559-45-0

CONTENTS

Editorial   7

Michael Ballin and Charles Lock (eds)
The Correspondence of James Purdy and John Cowper Powys 1956-1963   13

Jonathan Goodwin
Animated Fictions: Characters in *The Brazen Head*   115

Arjen Mulder
Into the World and Back Again: Reading Llewelyn Powys for the 21st Century   136

Alyse Gregory
The Limitations of the English Mind   161

Joel Hawkes (ed.)
Mary Butts (Re)viewing Llewelyn Powys's Dorset   167

Jeremy Hooker
St Peter and St Paul, Mappowder   175

REVIEW

Jeremy Hooker
Under the Shadow of the Oath: A Selection from the African Journals of Mary Casey
LOUISE DE BRUIN (ed.)   177

REVIEW-ESSAY
Charles Lock
Women's Writing: the Ways and Wiles of Obscurity   183

Patterns on the Sand
GAMEL WOOLSEY, with an introduction by Barbara Ozieblo

A Cage for the Nightingale
PHYLLIS PAUL, with an introduction by Glen Cavaliero

With the Hunted: Selected Writings
SYLVIA TOWNSEND WARNER, edited by Peter Tolhurst

Advisory Board   192
Notes on Contributors   192

Photograph of James Purdy taken by Carl Van Vechten on 15 March 1957, reproduced courtesy of the Beinecke Library, Yale University, and by permission of the Carl Van Vechten Trust. Under Van Vechten's will all income from his work, including the fee charged for this reproduction, is donated to the James Weldon Johnson Memorial Collection of Negro Arts and Letters.

EDITORIAL

In the last decade of his life John Cowper Powys was nominated for the Nobel Prize: though not substantiated as fact, it is a well-established myth. Of the distinguished figures invited to make nominations, the one responsible has never been securely identified. Of the obvious names — G.R. Wilson Knight, J.B. Priestley, Angus Wilson, for example — none owned up, nor claimed credit for the attempt. To this riddle that has provoked much musing over the decades, we now have the answer, and it is an unlikely one. The person who nominated John Cowper for the Nobel Prize in Literature was, in James Purdy's words, 'a very great British woman of letters': Dame Edith Sitwell.

Hitherto, the two most conspicuous families in twentieth-century English literature appear to have had little in common apart from the quantity of brothers and sisters in print. There is also the Derbyshire connection, Renishaw Hall lying across the Peak District from Shirley, and that sort of topographical affinity might have encouraged what John Cowper in the *Autobiography* confessed to being an unlikely admiration: 'I am capable of getting a good deal more pleasure than anyone would guess from difficult and sophisticated writers. I have in my time ... got lovely satisfaction from the delicate works of Sacheverell and Osbert Sitwell'. Elsewhere Powys expresses appreciation for Edith's poetry.

The person who drew Dame Edith's attention to John Cowper was the American novelist James Purdy (1914-2009), who has seldom figured at all in the Powys story. Purdy found a publisher in Britain through the efforts of Dame Edith Sitwell and John Cowper, to each of whom — for reasons not entirely clear — he had sent a copy of his first published story. Both responded with enthusiasm and lasting dedication.

Between 1957 and 1961 Powys and Purdy wrote to each other letters of admiration and encouragement. In doing so they uncovered numerous points of common interest and shared history. Powys reminisced about Greenwich Village in his day; some of his old friends were known to Purdy, among them Carl Van Vechten (1880-1964), the most prominent white supporter of the Harlem Renaissance and author of the controversial novel *Nigger Heaven* (1926). In the 1930s Van Vechten took up photography; he made a series of portraits of James Purdy in 1957-58, one of which serves as the frontispiece to this volume. Powys and Purdy discovered that they had in Gamel Woolsey a friend in common, and they were somewhat bemused to realize that they shared a French translator, Marie Canavaggia, who — during the course of these letters — was being asked to suspend her work on Powys's *Autobiography* in order to satisfy Gallimard's demand that she translate the next Purdy novel.

The significance of this correspondence, held in the Beinecke Library at Yale University, was first identified some years ago by Richard Maxwell. At that time he and Michael Ballin asked James Purdy for permission to publish the letters in the *Powys Journal*. Purdy refused, and it may be supposed that that refusal had nothing ill-intentioned about it but attested to the wish to protect his privacy: some of us on reading them would surely have rushed to interview him. Purdy's refusal may also point to the particular unguardedness of these letters. Following his death in 2009, the executors of Purdy's estate have kindly granted permission to the *Powys Journal* to print the letters; both sides of the correspondence are here published in full.

2014 will mark the centenary of Purdy's birth. In anticipation, two volumes of his writings are being published this year, with others to follow. Liveright/ W.W. Norton are issuing the newly-edited *Complete Short Stories of James Purdy* (containing all stories previously published, together with some hitherto never seen) and re-issuing one of his most controversial novels, *Cabot Wright Begins*, first published in 1964, the novel that Purdy was working on when Powys died.

The extent of this correspondence means that this volume of the *Powys Journal* contains fewer articles than usual. The one essay on John Cowper concerns a novel completed just before he was first contacted by Purdy; Jonathan Goodwin offers a most revealing analysis of *The Brazen Head* (1956) in which he brings out its continuities with the novels written decades earlier: this essay should draw readers back to an overlooked historical romance which, according to Goodwin's reading, discloses the very principles of John Cowper's art.

Each year the Editor must plead for submissions on other Powyses than John Cowper, and the call is repeated here. It is a special pleasure to publish Arjen Mulder's elegant defence of Llewelyn Powys as a writer, a defence that is both enthusiastic and analytically measured; one also that deals openly with the contrary view. This is a provocative piece, and we must hope that Llewelyn's writings will enjoy new readers, whether in admiration or detraction. One reader of long ago, mildly detracting, was the *Sunday Times* reviewer of Llewelyn's essays, the once-forgotten modernist, Mary Butts. Her two reviews have been recuperated and edited by Joel Hawkes. Mary Butts was brought up on the shores of Poole Harbour, and these reviews raise interesting questions of contiguity and contact — the literary custodians of Poole Harbour and Chaldon Herring seem to have been quite ignorant of each other — and indeed of rival claims to territorial ownership by memory and recreation. In the light of Arjen Mulder's discussion of Alyse Gregory we are reprinting an essay of hers that first appeared in the *Adelphi* in 1939; its theme, 'The Limitations of the English Mind', may be supposed to hold perennial interest.

The isolation of Chaldon Herring — and of Mappowder — may not be unrelated to the ways of the most eminent resident of both villages, T.F. Powys, described here in a newly-published poem as

>a man
>on no map known to us

As well as offering a poem, Jeremy Hooker reviews *Under the Shadow of the Oath: A Selection from the African Journals of Mary Casey*. This augments the essay on the poetry of Mary and Gerard Casey that Jeremy Hooker contributed to Volume XXII, and confidently assumes that Mary Casey is a poet and diarist of lasting power: we read her journals not only because of her celebrated uncles, but because she is herself manifestly, in every word penned, a writer.

John Cowper recommended to James Purdy the novels of Phyllis Paul, especially *Rox Hall Illuminated* which 'like your own writing ... shows some subtle demonic-angelic influence emanating from Edgar Allen Poe'. It may be through some such subtle influence that the works of Phyllis Paul are at last coming back into print: the Sundial Press has just issued *A Cage for the Nightingale* with a new foreword by

Glen Cavaliero. The Society's President was himself directed by John Cowper towards Phyllis Paul almost sixty years ago; in 1984, in the *Powys Review*, he discussed her work and John Cowper's enthusiasm for it, and now can we put those claims to the test. The same press has published for the first time *Patterns on the Sand*, an early novel by Gamel Woolsey, friend of both Purdy and Powys, and often mentioned in their letters. These two, together with a volume of Sylvia Townsend Warner's collected essays, are the subject of a review-essay by the Editor.

Powys and Purdy found that they were competing, through the publisher Gallimard, for the favours in translation of Marie Canavaggia, who in 1965 was able to add *Autobiographie* to the list of John Cowper's works available in French. Marcella Henderson-Peal has recently discovered in various French archives extensive evidence of an intense yet hitherto undetected degree of interest in Powys displayed by some of the most celebrated intellectuals of the age: Simone de Beauvoir, Gaston Bachelard, Raymond Queneau, Georges Bataille, Gabriel Marcel, among others. The fascinating and long overdue story of John Cowper's reception in France will be told in Volume XXIV.

John Cowper Powys on his couch at 1 Waterloo

John Cowper Powys in 1914, the year James Purdy was born

The Correspondence of James Purdy and John Cowper Powys 1956-1963

edited with an introduction by Michael Ballin and Charles Lock

Introduction

The correspondence between John Cowper Powys and the American novelist James Purdy (1914-2009) began in October 1956 and ended in February 1963. Powys was drawing towards the very end of his long life; he was writing *Homer and the Aether* and the fantasies, *Up and Out*, *The Mountains in the Moon* and *Real Wraiths*. In his secluded life with Phyllis Playter in North Wales, Powys was far from the world yet remarkably well informed. One of the few 'events' in those years was, in 1958, the visit to Blaenau Ffestiniog by a delegation of the Hamburg Free Academy of the Arts, on the occasion of Powys being awarded its Bronze Plaque.

James Purdy was, like Powys, a late starter as a writer of fiction. Raised in Ohio, educated at the University of Chicago, he moved, during this correspondence, from Pennsylvania to New York City; aged forty-two, he was only at the start of his literary career. His short story collection *63: Dream Palace* had been published in 1956; Purdy sent copies to an unlikely pair of writers in Britain, John Cowper Powys and Edith Sitwell, both of whom responded with enthusiasm. It was Sitwell who ensured that *63: Dream Palace* would be published in England, in 1960, by Victor Gollancz. This short novel (or long story) had been privately printed, on its own, in 1956 and re-issued in 1957, together with the stories of *Don't Call Me by My Right Name* (also privately printed in 1956), under the title *Color of Darkness: eleven stories and a novella*. This volume bears a dedication to Dame Edith Sitwell. The publisher was James Laughlin's New Directions in New York; the jacket carried endorsing words by, among others, John Cowper Powys, Langston Hughes, Marianne Moore, Sybil Thorndike and Angus Wilson. In 1961, as *Colour of Darkness*, these stories were published by Secker and Warburg, with an introduction for British readers by the dedicatee, Dame Edith Sitwell.

Dame Edith assures us that she is not alone in her admiration of James Purdy:

> As Mr. John Powys said of him, 'James Purdy is the best kind of original genius of our day. His insight into the diabolical cruelties and horrors that lurk all the time under our conventional skin is as startling as his insight into the angelic tenderness and protectiveness that also exist in the same hiding-place. Few there be that recognize either of these things. But Purdy reveals them.' (Edith Sitwell, Preface to James Purdy, *Colour of Darkness*, Secker and Warburg, 1961, 9)

Purdy's first novel, *Malcolm,* appeared in 1959 and *The Nephew* — dedicated to John Cowper Powys — in 1961. *Cabot Wright Begins* had been begun but not completed before Powys's death in June 1963; it was published in 1964. In circumstances, age and environment the two writers may have had little in common, yet through their letters they discovered many affinities, not least through Purdy's New York prompting Powys's recollections of the city fifty years earlier. Purdy and Powys never met.

Though his early novels were published by Farrar, Straus & Cudahy, Purdy enjoyed the loyalty and support of no single American publisher. His reception in Britain — Angus Wilson was another eminent admirer — was never quite matched by that in America. One of Purdy's early supporters in New York, Carl Van Vechten, had been known to Powys in his Greenwich Village days; it may have been Van Vechten who first suggested to Purdy that he write to Powys. Yet while Purdy is little read in Britain today, his recent admirers have included Susan Sontag and Gore Vidal; among the best-known of his younger advocates is Jonathan Franzen.

A recurring theme in this correspondence is the problem of censorship. The trial of Penguin Books for the publication of *Lady Chatterley's Lover* took place in October 1960, and Purdy had reason to be worried about his own transgressive themes and language. A four-letter word had imperilled the publication of *Lady Chatterley's Lover*; the use of 'motherfucker' had (to Purdy's annoyance) been deemed inappropriate by Victor Gollancz, in other respects a champion of liberal views. The elderly Dame Edith and John Cowper were quite unperturbed, and were themselves irritated by Gollancz's caution. In theme, the open presentation of homosexuality in Purdy's fiction created a serious problem in the period bounded in Britain by the publication of the Wolfenden Report in 1957 and the passing of the Sexual Offences Act in 1967. The characterization of Purdy as 'a homosexual writer' by the journalist Tom Hopkinson was the occasion for John Cowper to write a letter to the *Observer* in Purdy's defence; it was published on 14 July 1957. The discussion of this issue in these letters shows the two writers sharing a dislike for the categorizing that ignores individual particularities; they agree about the naturalness and diversity of sexuality as of personality.

It is remarkable how rapidly an affectionate warmth and psychological closeness develop from the polite and open but rather formal style of the first few letters: formalities of address quickly give way to 'my dear Jim' and 'your old pal'. The correspondents pledge eternal friendship to each other, and Purdy finds in Powys a mentor, a model and a protector. While Purdy presents himself as apprentice to the older writer, Powys is by no means always willing to act as sage. The reader gains a sense that Purdy's letters were eagerly awaited for the warmth and stimulation they brought into the remoteness of North Wales, not least their being sent from New York. Powys was a reluctant mentor, content rather to be seen as a struggling fellow-writer, still with much to learn. He tells Purdy that he and Phyllis 'never forget all that you and nobody else but you have done for our experience of life by yes! All you have <u>told</u> us and <u>explained</u> to us. The part you have played in our life my friend has been great' (November 5, 1961).

Purdy's letters recalled to Powys his youthful and energetic days in America during his career as an itinerant lecturer. Powys knew all the places known to Purdy, among them Pennsylvania, Ohio, Chicago and New York — especially Greenwich Village. And, of course, for Phyllis Playter the correspondence would have occasioned many American reminiscences. The two letter-writers also encouraged each other in their work: Purdy was beginning his literary career, and Powys was embarking at his advanced age on a new experimental vein of fantasy writing which elicited an anxiety that he shared with Purdy: 'but perhaps my excellent publishers will not want to publish these crazy books' (April 17, 1959). The letters also disclose some serendipitous personal connections; they had friends in common: Gerald Brenan and Gamel Woolsey were already known to Purdy. As well as their friendship with Carl Van Vechten in New York, in Paris Powys and Purdy discovered that they had the same French translator, Marie Canavaggia; both were deeply appreciative of her and her sisters.

For all his years in America Powys was deeply rooted in the nineteenth century, in the Britain of the Brontës, of Scott and of Hardy. Purdy writes within a distinctively American tradition of Hawthorne and Melville, Faulkner and Sherwood Anderson. His stories reveal the destructive and alienating features of modern life. Harsh realism does not preclude a distinctively surreal quality. In praising *Malcolm* Powys invokes the spirit of Emily Brontë as a point of reference for what he describes as 'the weird sexuality' of the novel. Yet in praising the spirit of 'horror and terror and pity' in Purdy's work, Powys recognizes its kinship with Edgar Allen Poe (June 29, 1957). The title of Purdy's early story collection *63: Dream Palace,* with its contrast between the specificity of the number and the name of the place — and a colon where we expect a comma — indicates its weird juxtapositions of the naturalistic and the grotesque. *Malcolm* is peopled with diversely eccentric characters negotiating between the extremes of realism and fantasy. Powys himself compares Purdy not only (almost inevitably) to Dickens but, much more interestingly, to their contemporary, Phyllis Paul (1903-73), a neglected writer much valued by Powys.

Purdy's realism exposes the disenchantment and bitterness of modern metropolitan life in the United States. The grim quality of Purdy's dramatization of suffering and alienation makes him a more obviously radical writer than Powys, yet it aligns him with Powys's close friend, the greatest of American realists, Theodore Dreiser. Yet Powys does not entirely exclude the dark aspects of modern life and the human heart alienated by the modern city: Wolf Solent's 'malice dance', for example, and the face on the Waterloo steps. Powys makes his own explorations of those 'diabolical cruelties and horrors' that he had recognized at once in Purdy's work. Both Powys and Purdy can distress the critics by mixing or even confusing the comic and the serious. Dorothy Parker judged *Malcolm* to be an outstandingly comic book, and the blurb for *Malcolm* cites Lilian Hellman: 'A brilliantly comic book'. The same advertisement quotes John Cowper Powys: 'A unique work of genius … . The tale floats and rocks like a boat on the mysterious river of which none of us really knows either the beginning or the end, the river of human life upon this earth.'

This correspondence reveals the close affection and sympathy between two writers who shared a sense of tradition and learning. Purdy was studying Greek, and could appreciate the subtleties in

Powys's *Homer and the Aether*, published in 1959; he was devoted to Arthurian lore and admired *A Glastonbury Romance*. But he was also enthusiastic about the *Autobiography* and the late fantasies, written in the years of this correspondence. Edith Sitwell says of Purdy: 'His work has great variety.' The same might be said of Powys. Both are able to create ordinary worlds of domestic and urban life, with characters whose prosaic destinies are redeemed only by their capacity for fantasy and illusion. *The Nephew*, dedicated to John Cowper Powys, suggests a significant influence. In the decades that followed this correspondence Purdy did his part in promoting John Cowper, notably in 1984 when Harper & Row attempted to relaunch Powys for American readers with paperback editions of *A Glastonbury Romance* and *Weymouth Sands*; the former carries an introduction by Robertson Davies, the latter, one by James Purdy.

This exchange, exclusively in letters, between two writers at such different stages in their lives is of more than documentary interest; we can witness each of them creatively shaping a living relationship out of nothing more than those thin sheets once recommended for airmail letters.

———————

Powys's use of exclamation marks and single, double and even triple underlinings has been reproduced as far as is practicable. Punctuation has been lightly supplied where it might be helpful. In order to conserve space, and so as to present the entire correspondence in a single issue of the *Powys Journal*, it has been necessary sometimes to gather independent sentences into paragraphs, and consistently to condense the often generous spacing of the salutations.

Powys always wrote by hand, in a hand at whose firmness and clarity Purdy often marvels; Purdy typed his letters. Although type offers less leeway than manuscript for an editor, punctuation has been silently amended and errors corrected, unless the error itself seems to be of significance.

Powys's letters are all written from the same address:

1 Waterloo
Blaenau-Ffestiniog
Merionethshire
North Wales
Great Britain

This heading, or a variant thereof, is present on almost every letter from Powys; here the address has been omitted throughout. All headings to Purdy's letters have been reproduced in full, though set on a single line.

Acknowledgments

The Estate of James Purdy has kindly given permission for the *Powys Journal* to publish Purdy's letters to Powys. These are held in the Beinecke Rare Book and Manuscript Library of Yale University, by whom permission has also been granted. For permission to publish Powys's letters the *Powys Journal* acknowledges the Beinecke Library and the Estate of John Cowper Powys. The Purdy Estate has also allowed us to reproduce Carl Van Vechten's photograph of James Purdy. The editors thank Pamela Malpas of Harold Ober Associates, representative of the James Purdy Estate, for her advice and assistance.

This project owes its inception to the late Richard Maxwell who made us aware of the existence of the Powys-Purdy correspondence at Yale University's Beinecke Library.

Chronological List of the Letters

The Beinecke Library holds 68 letters from Powys to Purdy and 35 letters from Purdy to Powys, distributed over the following years, and assigned numbers specifically for the present publication:

- 1956 Powys to Purdy 1-5
- 1957 Powys to Purdy 6-29
  Purdy to Powys 1-12
- 1958 Powys to Purdy 30-38
  Purdy to Powys 13-16
- 1959 Powys to Purdy 39-51
  Purdy to Powys 17-18
  Powys to Lynn Caine
- 1960 Powys to Purdy 52-59
  Purdy to Powys 19-26
- 1961 Powys to Purdy 60-67
  Purdy to Powys 27-32
- 1962 Powys to Purdy 68
  Purdy to Powys 33-34
- 1963 Purdy to Powys 35

The correspondence is not complete. Clearly, Purdy kept all those he received from Powys but did not retain copies of all his own. Some of the letters from Purdy that Powys actually received may well be extant. There is one letter here that does not belong to the correspondence: that dated 12 July 1959 and addressed to Farrar, Straus & Cudahy's Director of Publicity, Lynn Caine, who presumably — after selecting a few phrases to be used for publicity — passed it on to Purdy.

THE LETTERS

1956   Powys to Purdy 1-5

[*Powys to Purdy 1*]
October 28, 1956

My dear Mr. James Purdy,
   I am simply thrilled by these tales of yours.[1] I think they are wonderful, I think they are works of real genius. Aye! How I like them all! I couldn't stop reading them! I think you understand ladies' minds & ways as very few men do … I used to know Allentown ever so well, probably before you were born! I used to stop there on my lecturing journeys from Philadelphia to Pittsburg. In my old age I am, as old gents are only too apt to do, losing my memory, for I can't recall whether it was at Allentown or earlier in my journey from Philadelphia that I used to change for <u>Scranton</u> where I first heard the Wireless and for Wilkes-Barre.
   yrs ever J.C. Powys

There used to be a Welsh newspaper & more than one <u>Welsh Chapel</u>! Little did I think <u>then</u> that one day I'd find myself in Wales looking out words in a Welsh Dictionary! How destiny, my dear Mr. Purdy, does take us along in <u>circular curves</u> to our own end![2]

[*Powys to Purdy 2*]
Sunday Nov 25, 1956

My dear friend
   for in the subtlest of all aesthetic senses you sure are just that, I do thank you for Dream Palace wh. I shall read. I can see just as [I] have done [in] your other set [of] tales with what to an industrious old sod like me is the most exciting in a newly discovered writer namely a new fresh startling original way of describing ordinary home life in parlour & study & kitchen & street and pub and garden. I tell you I learn something fresh sans cesse while I read you. Your own J C Powys

[*Powys to Purdy 3*]
[undated: postmark Dec 26 1956]

O Yes my friend '63 Dream Palace' is just as unique as your other one. I think you belong to the class of writers who are for the future & in the future alone they will find their true appreciation. Think how they told Keats to go back to gallipots and how Donne now regarded (though <u>not</u> by a prejudiced old Tennysonian like me for I think that Cowper whom my great grandfather helped like a son and whose sonnet to him said 'Be wiser thou like our forefather Donne' was a far greater poet than Donne) as a poet almost as great as Milton and greater than Dryden neither of whose sandals in my opinion he was worthy to lick – felt he was done for when he eloped and wrote 'John Donne Ann Donne <u>undone</u>' which certainly was honest enough!

   I think myself that it is your knowledge of the feminine heart and its heights of heavenliness and its cavernous depths of horrible abominable evil worse than our male evil but <u>not simple</u> like our sadism and masochism O much more subtle & convoluted! Yes I think you are a great and profound understander of human hearts and nerves especially <u>feminine ones</u> beyond any psychiatrist or any psychologist who thinks he's scientific! O I <u>know</u> I'm right in this, yes they are afraid of you because <u>ladies are the chief readers of modern books</u> and you reveal their secret feeling and nervous reactions and diabolical wickedness!
Well I must stop! Good luck to you my <u>friend</u>. Your faithful admirer JC Powys.

[*Powys to Purdy 4*]
Woden's Day Dec 19 1956

<u>Hurrah!</u> <u>Congratulations!</u> I am <u>so glad</u>! Yes! I wrote exactly the few sentences he wanted for this admirable man (aye but I do <u>so</u> admire him!) Mr Victor <u>Gollancz</u>[3] <u>from your intense admirer</u> my dear James P. <u>John C P</u>
   She has insight our Dame Edith Sitwell

[*Powys to Purdy 5*]
[Undated Air Letter 1956]

O my dear James P.
what you tell of <u>Dame Edith Sitwell</u> is grand news. I <u>adore</u> that lady! She and Dr Edith Starkie[4] of Oxford are my two <u>Egerias</u> or 'Nymphae in Antro' like the <u>original Egeria</u> – who helped king Numa establish Rome – quite <u>independently</u> of those wolf cubs Romulus and Remus! Miss Sitwell and Miss Starkie are both wonderful. I do not know either personally but I worship them from afar. Both have <u>Edith</u> as their name.

1957   Powys to Purdy 6-29
   Purdy to Powys 1-12

[*Powys to Purdy 6*]
Tuesday, January 8, 1957

This is only a scrawl, my dear James <u>not</u> to be answered but I've found a modern English writer a Miss I am sure – these misses ever since Egeria the Nymph in the cave who helped King Numa to found Rome are the ones! Maiden Aunties are what all we kids need! Do try and get from some library this Book – 'Rox Hall Illuminated' by <u>Phyllis Paul</u> and published by <u>Heinemann</u>.[5] Like your own writing it shows some subtle demonic-angelic influence emanating from Edgar Allen Poe and especially to be found as Thomas Hardy himself taught me in '<u>Ulalume</u>'. There's a maiden lady like this in Oxford today who dominates all the Dons, <u>Dr Enid Starkie</u>, who made them give degrees to André Gide and quite lately to Jean Cocteau. O I do pray you will get a chance of seeing the One we are fellow-worshippers of, namely Dame Edith. I've never seen her but I know there's nobody like her!

   No answer to this scrawl, mind – but we won't <u>ever</u> stop corresponding!
   Your old <u>Jack Powys</u>

[*Powys to Purdy 7*]
Friday, January 25 1957

My dear Jim

 Yes it's really very queer how we've made friends without ever meeting. But I feel we've got each other's number to a T. And this is proved by our adoration so entirely mutual for these Noble Dames who are all 'Nymphs in Antro' like Numa's Egeria. Aye! But I am so thrilled at these words about me & all my literary labours from my grand Heroine Dame Edith. No I don't know Dame Sybil Thorndike but she must be what you say.

 Phyllis Paul has written several novels but this <u>Rox Hall</u> one is absolutely <u>terrifying</u>! I finished reading it aloud the day before yesterday. She is a puzzle to me – I wrote to her once and she answered to my letter politely but by some <u>psychometric spirit</u> emanating from [her] letter (if <u>that</u> is the right word) I got the feeling she doesn't want to be praised by anyone. She writes to write and she must until we are all turned to dust. I['d] give a lot to know whether she is a Roman Catholic. Dame Edith and Doctor Enid are much too wise to <u>be</u> anything. But Phyllis Paul might I feel (like the angels and devils) easily take the form of either St Augustine or, or someone else! She is deadly subtle – any of her books would give <u>you</u> well! an idea of her. She's a little like <u>I Compton Burnett</u> whose face – I've <u>never seen</u> her face before today in some paper – is awe-inspiring. I used to think that 'I' meant <u>ego</u> or <u>moi</u> but it stands for <u>Ivy</u>! Yes, I <u>can</u> see <u>where the sea is</u>, but I doubt if I've ever seen the actual <u>water</u> of it, from the road up up up that I take daily – <u>Port Madoc</u> is the nearest <u>sea-side town</u> from whence the Welsh Prince Madoc discovered America long before the Vikings.

 O I do agree about the Sea – my father's mother as a widow lived for years & *years* at Weymouth and tho' the first five of us were born at Shirley Vicarage in Derbyshire we went <u>all of us all our lives</u> down to the sea at Weymouth and Portland in Dorset – O I agree!

 I shall now be struggling with Homer's Iliad and this wonderful Dictionary translated from the German: Autenrieth's Homeric Dictionary published by <u>Macmillan</u> in New York in <u>1902</u> <u>translated by</u>

a Mr Keep. No I never drink anything now but milk and tea. I can tell you my exact diet for every single day: 2 bottles of milk, 2 pots of tea 3 raw eggs and 4 mouthfuls of dry, stale, white bread.
Well! All the best to you, Jim from your old Jack.

[*Powys to Purdy 8*]
Tuesday, February 5

My dear Jim

Yes you & I suit each other perfectly. O I love to think of Dame E going for you over Dame S. That's where ladies are so much more unguarded & natural than us males who can never never never never never forget our Dignity! In our heart of hearts we males are all actors on a little ideal stage with only two persons to form the audience. What Persons. Number one ourself and Number two all other living things in the universe fused into one which you can think of as Nature or Humanity or God just as you like as long as it includes every possible Weigher Appraiser Judge Observer Passer-by and Loiterer or Conscious Audience at our Performance. This feeling of being actors on a stage with Ourself in Balcony & the All-Embracing Other in the Stalls never leaves us men. But our ladies have only to feel – and they forget both the One in the Balcony and the Other in the Stalls and just burst out! This is the tragic comedy of all Marriages – Mr always watching himself and being watched by the All and Mrs saying what she feels at the moment – 'O you great Clumsy Lout!' But as long as man can cry like Othello: 'Excellent Wretch! Perdition catch my soul if I don't love you!' all will be well to the end ... But it's interesting to note that some traveller in the Middle East tells us that the Egyptians thought Iago was meant to be the Hero of that Play!

No I've never read, never even heard of La Celestina.[6] But I'll tell you what book I'm enjoying now & reading aloud to my lady-friend: 'The Borrowers' by Mary Norton and illustrated by Diana Stanley.[7] I've begun its sequel today 'The Borrowers Afield' it's the sort of book that everybody who reads it knows that it will live forever & so calls it a classic – it's a child's book for adults especially for an adult in Second childhood – ever your Old Jack.

[*Powys to Purdy 9*]
March 21 1957

My dear Jim,

O I am so thrilled that you met our great goddess that we both admire so much. I value the work of both her brothers but I think she's the greatest of the family & I was so pleased at her sending me her blessing and commendation. Your description of her tallies with what I feel about her & have long felt.

Don't ee forget my dear Jim the names of those two favourite lady writers of mine if ever you are looking thro' the shelves of a lending library: <u>Mary Norton</u> author of 'The Borrowers' and its sequel <u>The Borrowers Afield</u>. Over here these books only cost three shillings and sixpence each. And <u>Phyllis Paul</u> author of 'Camilla' – 'The Lion of Cooling Bay' – and 'Rox Hall Illuminated'. As to that final word that our goddess got angry with the Publisher for cutting out;[8] I've got a weird & eccentric interest in another side-line of what the Christian tradition which haunts us so (though it doesn't burn us at the stake as it used to do) shrinks from with such dark and shivering horror, namely the incestuous feeling of brothers & sisters [for] each other. Our heads are now full of Egypt because of the Canal but I've been thinking of the Egypt from which Abraham escaped, by the help of Jehovah's Thunder, carrying Sarah with him. I don't think Sarah was Abraham's sister but she certainly would have served one Pharaoh in place of another if Jehovah hadn't thundered! For it was the rigid and ritualistic and <u>unalterable</u> custom for Pharaohs to marry their sisters.

Well! I must stop. But O O O! How difficult it is to stop writing to friends. However! We've all got our job. So good luck! Ever your old Jack.

[*Powys to Purdy 10*]
Saturday April 13, 1957

Aye! Jim my dear how glad I am to hear your words of praise for my old Autobiography. O & I am longing for you to read my Rabelais too – I was helped with the most difficult part of it by another of these wonderful British ladies. I speak now of Dr. Enid Starkie of Oxford who by her wisdom compelled the Oxford authorities to give Monsieur Gide and Monsieur Cocteau of France, <u>Oxford Degrees</u>! She made the great Book Shop in Oxford send me the Giant of my Book-shelf namely Four great volumes of <u>Littré's</u> French-French dictionary!! But O how I do share & rejoice in your worship of Dame Edith! I keep a picture of her ever so sacredly!

Yes I shall and My American Lady-friend will too you can bet your life look out every word in the papers about Gollancz's (O I do admire Gollancz so much!) Edition of your Work! You shall hear what we pick up & we pick up a lot you can imagine! What I am doing now is a considerably long and very very daring book on Homer's Iliad, not a translation tho' I have to translate a lot incidentally but a sort of a paraphrase in which I imagine the thoughts and feelings not only of the great heroes like Hector and Achilles but of the <u>immortal gods</u> in their Olympian heaven!! especially the feelings of <u>Zeus</u> their boss which gives me a grand opportunity indirectly to have a few passing shots at the great one known in our religion as <u>GOD</u>! Well! I must return now to my Iliad of Homer.

Yrs ever Jack – J C Powys

O no – I can't speak a word of Welsh nor could my Father nor <u>his</u> Father who was one of the chief Bosses of Corpus Christi College Cambridge where Christopher Marlowe was an undergraduate. But my Father always used to tell us that we are descended thro' the barons of Maen-Y-Meifod from Rhodric Mawr King of Wales!!![9] and certainly it is a definite historic fact that one of the three Provinces of Wales or Cymru was called Powys. The other two historic provinces of Wales were Gwyneth and Deheubarth.

[*Powys to Purdy 11*]
Monday, April 15, 1957

My dear Jim,

Phyllis my American lady from Kansas shares my admiration for you & is anxious to tell you how thrilled we both are by these <u>two</u>

photographs of 'your wone self' as we say in Dorset! And taken too by an Artist for whom in 'Greenwich Village' as we called it when we lived in Patchin Place we had such a great reverence and respect.[10] We have propped them up pro tem anyway on the shelf among my preciousest books in this upper chamber where I lie on my Couch by the window reading & writing, the full-face one with its back to Walt Whitman's poetry and the other with its back to the terribly tattered volume of Shakespeare's plays and you bet I give a regular lecture on you to all our favourite visitors!

But by Jehovah and Pallas Athene my favourite deities I wish by the waters of the Styx that we had no visitors except our very very very most favourite ones! I am sending you or we are, as she's the one as takes it to the Post – a new translation of the old Welsh stories about Merlin and Arthur etc etc etc in a new translation by a friend of mine called Glyn Jones[11] & a friend of his, professors in the Welsh college of Aberystwyth. The best of translations of this weird savage book is the one made by Lady Charlotte Guest whose maiden name was Lindsey who was the daughter of an English Earl.

When Guest died – who was an iron worker with huge iron works at a place called Dowlais in mid Wales – Lady Charlotte ran these great Iron Works employing thousands of Welshmen for 10 years herself. Then she married a learned man I fancy, but I don't know, a German who was her daughter's Tutor and when both he & old Guest had been long dead she had herself driven in a carriage all over Europe collecting China and her collection was so much the best ever made that when at last she died in old age it was given to the British Museum! There's a lady for you! And she was more beautiful from all the pictures I've seen of her than any lady I have ever seen in my life.[12]

And now alas! Her version of the Mabinogion is out of print! This version which I am sending you by my friend Prof. Glyn Jones & his friend will at least give you some idea of the strangeness and weirdness of these extraordinary tales! Don't exhaust yourself with them if they seem too confusing and too queer; with their cumbrous & funny Welsh names because it's much more important that you should write more of your own books than spend time struggling with these crazy legends &

myths <u>but I did want you to see them</u>!!   ever and always your devoted Old Jack

Don't reply till you have received this queer Book & looked at it!

[*Powys to Purdy 12*]
Thursday, May 16, 1957

My dear Jim,

Aye! But I am so glad you like The Mabinogion & those names so much! I confess I am a little too old-fashioned in my taste in poetry to be able to do full justice to Dylan Thomas's actual poetry but I have always been absolutely carried away <u>by his voice</u>. I <u>have never heard</u> such a voice anywhere in the world. I heard his voice first in a description he gave of all the things they had in what was called 'the festival of Britain' [1951] and I have heard it since on the wireless <u>several times</u>, generally reading his own poetry. No I've <u>never</u> heard a <u>voice</u> that impressed me as much. And I've got a fondness for his very curious countenance – you will read about the original Dylan in the Mabinogion and of how when they took him to the sea to baptize him he turned into a fish and swam away & was never seen again!

I love to think of Carl Van Vechten (for whom we all in 'Greenwich Village' in New York had great admiration and respect)[13] and of his liking our T.F.P.'s <u>Mr Weston's Good Wine</u> best of all Novels! I always say to everybody who is interested in us eleven children of the Rev C.F. and Mrs. Mary Cowper Powys that Llewelyn is far the most loveable and attractive, Theodore far the most original, A.R.P. (Bertie the Architect) the most honest, and my old brother Littleton, with whom I was in the nursery and at school & college the wisest, and Johnny-Jack-John the cleverest! Now only I have one brother left – William E. Powys of Kenya who is certainly of us all the <u>Bravest</u>. He got some romantic-sounding Belgian honour in the first war. He has visited Phyllis & me when he came to London to sell his sheep-wool & was most interested in our Welsh sheep much more active climbing rocks than any others. He is very popular with the blacks in Kenya & has had no trouble from the Mau-Mau where he lives.

O my dear Jim it gives me such deep satisfaction that you like the idea of this audacious & presumptuous Homer's Iliad of mine. I've nearly done half of it!

Yr ever & aye – & Phyllis she do say the same – Jack
I enclose a speech on Modern Poetry by our Dame.

[*Powys to Purdy 13*]
Sat May 18 1957

My Dear Jim,

I'll obey you & not write a proper letter. This is only a scrawl to say how thrilled I am by learning of the pictures on your work table and also by to us both this most exciting news of your being a friend of Gerald and Gamel Brenan and of you liking his books.[14] Your ink is certainly wonderfully Black but I noticed no attar of Erebon! Yrs always & ever Jack

[*Powys to Purdy 14*]
June 6 1957

My dear Jim

O I think it was because I had made up my mind that it would be better for me not to bring <u>any</u> feminine person at all into that book and those I <u>did</u> bring in came <u>perforce</u> and of <u>necessity</u> as the story <u>had to bring them in</u> – to be a self-story at all!! Of course in reality I owe <u>everything</u> as all the eleven of us did – six boys and five girls – to our mother. My own particular debt to her was her love of poetry – <u>especially</u> of the poetry of <u>Tennyson</u>, I have now on my shelf '<u>Moxon's Selection from Tennyson</u>' the headlines to the poems all the way through are most exquisitely coloured by her. She taught me to read Tennyson's poems by heart and then repeat them or <u>recite</u> them to her and all this very soon made me a great learner by heart and reciter of poetry which helped me to earn my living lecturing in every state & nearly every big City in the U.S.A. for over 30 years!

No children could probably have had a wiser or a more sympathetic mother. She had a special '<u>corner</u>' as we say <u>with each of us</u>. With

John over Poetry, with Littleton over games, with Theodore over stoical philosophy under tribulation; but she concentrated on looking after our father and every evening would read to him. While we all occupied ourselves in a big 'school-room' or 'servants-hall' at the other end of the house with our own pursuits. 'My children' she would say to visitors 'like to be together.' And so we did. O I am so glad you heard from Dame Edith from her Renishaw house. I am so interested too to hear you have heard from Angus Wilson and Noel Coward. Yes and by heaven dear Jim, you can bet I'll be looking out for that long Review by our Dame E in the <u>Times Literary Sup. on yr Book</u>. Phyllis & I always see the Times Lit Sup. I see that July 1st is a Monday and as tomorrow is the 7th of June it is less than a month away now!

Yes I am getting near the end of Book XII of the Iliad and shall soon be starting on the Second Volume in this Heinemann and Putnam's Edition of the <u>Loeb Classical Library</u>.

We are both looking forward to the arrival of this short story of yours published in the New Yorker.[15] We shall be excited to see if we can discover a <u>bit more</u> of the <u>Demon</u> than the <u>tip of his ear & the tip of his tail</u>.

yrs always & P says too. <u>Jack</u>

[*Powys to Purdy 15*]
June 19 1957

My dear Jim

I'm already deep in your book [*63: Dream Palace*] sent me in anticipation of July 1st when it is to be officially published. Alas! You must forgive me dear Jim if while I enjoy reading it I am 'feeling my age' as Hardy used to say to me too much to be able to write an essay on it when it comes out. But I guess that with the support of our grand Dame 'as the Queen calls her' and your other champions of both sexes it will make a big hit on both sides of the Atlantic and this excellent <u>Gollancz</u> will feel well rewarded for being its Publisher.[16] yrs with all my heart Jack C Powys

[*Powys to Purdy 16*]
June 29 1957

O my dear Jim

I do pray the wonderful prayer all the <u>very old</u> hermits in Thibet pray:
    'Om mani
        Padme Hum'
tho' I don't know what it means, what it's for, or to what deity or deities it is addressed! But I <u>have</u> found that it can work a <u>magic spell</u> – and I pray that when <u>July 1st</u> arrives & your Book comes out from the Press of that excellent daring & liberal publisher Gollancz that it will have some wonderful reviews. I shall not alas! be able to write a review of it myself because I am getting tho' comfortable in body, more shaky in mind. O my dear Jim but I am <u>so pleased</u> you've got <u>that</u> money to go on with while you finish your novel <u>Malcolm</u>. This news makes me think of a long historical novel (in MSS <u>so far</u>) by my niece Mary Casey in Kenya East Africa called <u>Egbert</u> who was the grandfather of King Alfred. I pray that Gollancz or some equally good publisher will publish Malcolm [&] that my Mary's Egbert also find a publisher [-] for next Monday the day after tomorrow. Your loyal & faithful reader till death do us part John Cowper Powys.

[*Powys to Purdy 17*]
Monday July 1st

Well my dear Jim the day has come and has turned out well! In both our Papers there were Reviews of your Book and though word-critical here & there of unimportant points in sentence structure both reviews were pretty lengthy and both gave the gist of your work a most satisfactory means of recognition. Had it been on Poe himself it couldn't, <u>they</u> couldn't, the two my Miss Playter and I read, have given a more unqualified acknowledgment of your power and genius in creating this very <u>very special</u>, or shall I say in digging out of the human quarry this <u>special</u> vein of <u>horror and terror and pity</u> which – was it Aristotle who said those words 'purges the mind'. I do indeed and from the bottom of my heart my dear friend congratulate you – you certainly are now

recognized over here for what you are – a true inheritor of that [pure?] touch which – as Thomas Hardy told me when he first introduced me to <u>Ulalume</u> – was the unique possession of Edgar Allen Poe!   yours in triumph John Cowper Powys
I hope this stick is magic.

[*Purdy to Powys 1*]
439 Walnut Street, Apt 6, Allentown, Pennsylvania, USA
11 July, 1957

Dear dear Jack,

I hope you don't mind my writing you so often! I was so moved by your Prayer from Tibet that I must thank you for it, because I do so believe in those things, and in their magic! Thank you Jack, more than I can say for your kindness, your friendship, and your encouragement. They have meant so much to me in many dark moments!

Along with your picture & the beautiful MABINOGION, and your precious letters, I am terribly interested in your niece's EGBERT and do hope and pray she finds a publisher. There is almost nothing as fascinating as King Arthur, at least to me.

Jack, dear Jack, I have heard a bit here and a bit there about JULY 1, but it seems so far away, and maybe all a dream. I never dreamed when friends here published my little stories they would make dear friends in England! And now I have you, Dame Edith, Gerald Brenan and as you say that splendid courageous man, Victor Gollancz. I don't want to tire you with more, but want you to know I say a PRAYER for you each day, and may you keep strong and well and remember your loving friend. Jim

Speaking of Kenya: I once read a book by Isak Dinesen OUT OF AFRICA, which was very beautiful, I thought.

[*Powys to Purdy 18*]
July 11, 1957

O my dear Jim

Did I tell you that Gerald Brenan and his lovely and extremely intellectual & tender-hearted and original wife <u>Gamel</u> (née Wo[o]lsey)

Gamel Woolsey and John Cowper Powys

from America, are great friends of ours: I think Gamel is Phyllis's best friend. O my dear Jim Phyllis and your old Jack are both thrilled to think of you in New York City!! Somewhere in what we used to call Greenwich Village I hope. I believe our friend the poet E. E. Cummings has bought the whole of the house in Patchin Place where there is an Ailanthus Tree, & where we used to live on the top floor.

Think of your leaving Allentown at the end of this month! I wrote a savage letter in defence of your book to the Sunday Observer and I rather fancy from what Mr Gollancz said – O what a man he is! – I do admire him! – the critic who said your book was 'homo' 'implicit and explicit' may answer my furious letter this coming Sunday the 14th so it will be exciting to see![17] Yes! I adore our Dame Edith & it does my heart good to hear anytime about her.

Your old Jack

[*Purdy to Powys 2*]
439 Walnut, Apt. 6, Allentown, Pa. USA
July 14, 1957

My dear Jack,
[4 lines in Greek[18]]
I have tried to find in Homer a comment on the Event, and I do hope I have found the right one! I wanted to have a quotation from the book you are working on! You will note my Greek script is a bit on the amateur side. What I need is a Greek teacher!

Jack, I live here in the Negro slums and enjoy it, but I seem to have heard only from you from that far-off land ENGLAND, and I simply cannot believe they published me and that I am ESTABLISHED. I cannot even believe some times Dame Edith is REAL! I am all alone here and nobody even knows I write. THIS IS NOT A COMPLAINT. Jack, for your friendship and kindness and encouragement I can never thank you. My best wishes to you over all that ocean and land, my dear friend,

JIM

Redwood Anderson with John Cowper Powys

CORRESPONDENCE

[*Powys to Purdy 19*]
St Swithin's Day July 15 1957

My dear Jim

Yes our 'splendid' Mr Gollancz suggested that I should write a letter to <u>The Observer</u> one of our best <u>Sunday Papers</u> defending you from a criticism of your Book which was written by a Mr Tom Hopkinson of whom I knew Nothing. And I did write a savage, if perhaps a bit pedantic defence of your Book which sure enough appeared yesterday under the rather too startling headline <u>Desperate Cry</u>. This referred not to you <u>but to me</u>! & my 'desperate cry' was the expression of <u>indignation</u> because your critic didn't do you justice … I have a friend here in this neighbourhood for a month or two an old poet and his younger wife – John Redwood-Anderson and Gwyneth Anderson to whom my Miss Playter & I have just <u>lent your book</u> and I <u>know</u> they both will be thrilled by it! Gwyneth the wife <u>knows</u> Mr Tom Hopkinson! – whom I attacked a bit too indignantly with my 'desperate cry' & she tells us that he is [a] nice man so I hope I haven't been too violent but I am impulsive by nature and I did feel so strongly about it. She says she heard him when he lectured to Quakers so he <u>can't</u> be, any way, as violent & impetuous as I am! Both Miss Playter & I do <u>so long</u>, my dear, to learn where you <u>do finally decide to settle down in New York City</u>. So do tell us the moment it <u>is</u> hit upon – that hiding place! Aye! And I pray to the gods that your book <u>makes a real hit</u>.
   yours as you know Jack

Both Phyllis and Mrs Gwyneth Anderson know that Book by <u>Isak Dinesen</u> and they say that in spite of the name Isak she is a lady! I enclose my <u>'Desperate Cry' in case you haven't heard it!</u>

[*Powys to Purdy 20*]
July 19th 1957

My dear Jim,
   I think this is quite a good review of your Book – I think I cut it from the Daily Telegraph. It is by a writer called <u>Kenneth Young</u> who is I think quite excellent at his job though I don't know him. But I think

this article of his is very satisfactory & I wanted you to see it as soon as possible.

Yrs always Jack

[*Purdy to Powys 3*]
439 Walnut Street, Apt. 6, Allentown, Pennsylvania, USA
July 23, 1957

Dear Jack,

How very pleased I was to get your very good letter with the fine review of my stories by KENNETH YOUNG. I thought it was very good indeed, and both intelligent and fair. Of course he does not KNOW as much as you and Dame Edith!

I am packing to leave this old mountain fortress and go temporarily to New York City, but I hope soon to find a more <u>human</u> place, perhaps by that most calming and inevitable of all things THE SEA.

Do take care of yourself Jack. Dame Edith wrote me a very beautiful letter from Renishaw – she is going to London, she says, for August – her review of my book has not yet appeared in the TIMES LITERARY SUPPLEMENT. Jack, I do hope your book on HOMER is progressing fine – it is a book that I know will be, if possible, even greater than your RABELAIS.

My affectionate best wishes, and many many thanks for your kindness and interest, Your admirer & friend, always, <u>Jim</u>
I will stay here until August 1st.

[*Purdy to Powys 4*]
439 Walnut Street, Apt. 6, Allentown, Pennsylvania, USA
July 25, 1957

My dear Jack,

I just received from Victor Gollancz your spirited and noble defence of my book against Mr. Tom Hopkinson. Jack, apart from my deep gratitude, I DO <u>agree</u> WITH YOU, and WOULD, even if my book was not the occasion for this profound difference of viewpoint. You are absolutely right, I feel. Mr. Hopkinson consciously or unconsciously uses the word homosexual (God knows <u>what</u> that means!) to explain away his own guilty fear of the things I tried to portray! If we use the word <u>homosexual</u>, then Hamlet, Don Quixote, Oedipus Rex, the Iliad, Moby Dick, Leaves of Grass, Bouvard et Pecuchet, the Way of all Flesh, – all all are merely homosexual and therefore <u>nothing</u>! What drivel!

The fact is that the Freudians and their ilk are all at heart little petty bourgeois idiots who are as ashamed of common humanity as they are of themselves. They are horrified of the human, and with Freud are trying to get rid of it. And they seem to be succeeding. They would like to get rid of suffering, effort, love and pain so that they could all be these adjusted automata, sitting around having refined and happy thoughts. Well I believe in original sin, if not theologically, at least in FACT!

Those people that the English reviewers say – those people in my stories, that is, that they say are so loathsome are not loathsome at all to any <u>human</u> being. It is the reviewers that are always finding humanity loathsome when it is not merely petty bourgeois refinement.

Well that sounds like a Marxist, and I HATE Marxists, too. I HATE all these old intellectual frauds Freudians, Marxists, etc. They wont look at anything and they cant feel anything!

Oh, dear Jack, I hope I haven't worn you out with all this. Dame Edith and Victor Gollancz are so very proud of <u>you</u>, and they know your greatness. Anyhow I don't care what those reviewers say because I have you and Dame Edith and Victor Gollancz, and what MORE could I want.

God bless you, Jack, Every good wish to you, and my everlasting gratitude and ADMIRATION, Jim

I sent you a nice handkerchief to wipe your brow of the critics!

[*Powys to Purdy 21*]
July 29, 1957

My Dear Jim

I do indeed thank you for this beautiful and delicate handkerchief. I shall keep it as long as I live. And I thank you too for your gallant and world-defying letter! It's the sort of letter that any of our favourite great ones would sign & seal! Lord! What fools these mortals be! <u>Our loves and hates</u>, Jim old friend, certainly do seem to co-incide! I read lately in one of these papers – I never can remember <u>which one</u>! – a splendid article on our heroic Dame: saying she is the best poet & prophetess of our age in which I heartily concur. Why the devil don't they make her our <u>Poet Laureate</u>? But of course she may not outlive the present one – whoever he is! Masefield I think – but I may be wrong.[19]

Let me know won't you as soon as you've found your new retreat! Jack

[*Purdy to Powys 5*]
138 West 70th Street, Apt 3, New York City N.Y.
August 2, 1957

My dear Jack,

Far from finding your defense of my book 'pedantic' or 'emotional' I found it dignified, right to the point, and full of deep feeling. To use the word homosexual in the way Mr. Tom did is just as incendiary on the emotions of the average man as it was in Hitler's Germany to say <u>this work smacks of the Jew or in McCarthy's America to say this work has strong communist overtones</u> or in Franco's Spain to say <u>he is a Freemason in his point of view</u>. The word homosexual has a vast foggy meaning even in psychoanalysis but in the world of journalism it can only inflame prejudice. That is why this Mr Tom did it; he couldnt stand the book, and he wanted to defame it. He chose the most cowardly, most unmanly, most HOMOSEXUAL method. There is no doubt in my mind Mr Tom is either a practicing <u>fellator</u> or would like to be, and there isnt a particle of doubt in my mind he is ONE.

He completely ignored the sympathetic study in my book of women, and of the homosexual man in MAN AND WIFE. He also ignored everything else in my book except the feelings of guilt, fear and horror which the writing evoked in his own GUILT-TORTURED soul. He is a Philistine, a sneak, and a 'pious fraud'. These fake scientists who pronounce their fake medical and scientific terms on the innocent human beings they capture in their laboratories should in turn have to face the public they inflame. Mr T. should have to show photographs to the court of public opinion that his own organ has properly been in use of heterosexual society. (Perhaps these photos could be shown to the Quakers.) He should prove his manhood or to the Tower.

Well, forgive this diatribe!

Yes, sir, Jack I am on the way to old NEW YORK. I will leave about 8 or 9th, and I live right near BROADWAY.

I can't begin to tell you how much I have appreciated all your good letters, the clippings and YOUR FRIENDSHIP this year. These critics are all mad they weren't consulted BEFORE you and Dame Edith. They feel they were invited to the banquet table only after the preferred had dined, and it makes them terribly cross.

I am so pleased to know that you and your good friend Phyllis are friends [with] the Brenans. Why we all have a very strong bond in common!

I must go back to my packing!

Dear Jack, I will NEVER forget your friendship and your GENIUS. After reading A DESPERATE CRY, I read your AMERICA section in your AUTOBIOGRAPHY, and it is great; the description of the American and his mechanical skills is perfect, the best I ever read.
Your friend always Jim
Imagine what old Tom H would have said in the days Lucius Apuleius' Metamorphosis or Golden Ass appeared – about that strange old queer book! How, as you suggest do those lovely critics read those terrible old books without getting blisters on their tongues!

[*Powys to Purdy 22*]
Friday, August 9th 1957

Well my dear friend I long to hear how you feel in your new dwelling and what encounter good or bad or obscure or comic you have had with your neighbours and with the Officials or the landlords or the Overseers or queer persons Black or White or Red or Yellow Giants or Dwarfs of Goblins or Gnomes or Elves that you will have around you. And I want to hear how near you are to Central Park and in what direction you will walk when you feel a longing for air & exercise! At this moment Miss Phyllis Playter whose grandparents were Quakers is watching the Film about <u>Moby Dick</u>.[20] I long to learn how they deal with the great white whale in a modern Film! Yes indeed we <u>are</u> fast friends of the Brenans. Yes, indeed, let our critics read the Golden Ass!

Think of your actually opening this in West 70th St!!

always while I am alive your loyal old Jack

[*Purdy to Powys 6*]
138 West 70th Street, Apt 2 B, New York, New York
August 10, 1957

My dear Jack

Here I am in an entirely different world. It is just as much a 'melting pot' as ever, and I don't think they will ever get everybody 'melted' down here, which is good. It will be an awful day when they do get everybody MELTED!

Dear Jack will you think me an awful nuisance if I ask you to recommend me for a GUGGENHEIM fellowship for completing my novel MALCOLM. I don't think there will be any work in it for you, but you will just have to NOD your head (not in the Homeric sense) and I know those GUGGENHEIMS will be thrilled to hear from you even if it's only for you to say YES. I have nearly forgotten about the prig in the OBSERVER because there is so much to dazzle and confuse.

Carl Van Vechten has invited me for dinner to his house tonight, and I will tell you the news of that. He is very fond of you and of THEODORE. He often asks me for news of you.

Dear Jack, take care of yourself, and know I am thinking of you. Your devoted friend, <u>Jim</u>

[*Powys to Purdy 23*]
Tuesday, August 13 <u>1957</u>

Here today my dear Jim comes your First letter from your New dwelling. It is a very lucky day for me for it is the Birthday of my brother Llewelyn who was and is one of the most lovable of our family; though

Theodore was and is far the most original and my brother Littleton who died recently in his 80's far the most sensible and with far greatest knowledge of birds and butterflies and wild Nature. A Mr Coombes has been writing a life of Theodore I don't know for what publisher and he wrote to all of us asking <u>whether</u> Theodore went to Church and <u>why</u> he took Holy Communion.[21] Some of us answered that he went to Church <u>to be alone</u>, and took the Sacrament so as not to hurt the feelings of the clergyman. O yes! Of course I'll reply to Guggenheims when I hear from them 'in good set terms and motley' though I be.[22] O yes the name of Carl Van Vechten evokes many affectionate memories in my mind. Yes I long to hear more of your adventures among the <u>unmelted</u>!

Yrs as always Jack

[*Purdy to Powys 7*]
138 West 70th Street, Apt 2 B, New York 23, New York
August 14, 1957

My dear Jack,

How happy I was to see your good handwriting again, like a thing from home, because I am in this strange and bewildering monster city. I live just a ten minute walk East to Central Park, and a few minutes West brings me to the Hudson River. I am really in the slums again, just as I was in Allentown, and they are nearly all negroes and most of them seem to be from Puerto Rico and Cuba. There is one negress with a powerful hand (I only see her hand) who keeps a chicken which lives on her windowsill and I believe she is a witch. Perhaps the chicken is a person in disguise, or it may be the old black hag herself, as I never see her and the chicken together.

I went to see Carl Van Vechten last week, and he spoke of you, and we had a nice evening together talking and talking until Morning.

Then yesterday came a letter from Dame Edith. She said she became so ill from reading that man in the OBSERVER and that 'fool' (she called him) in the SUNDAY TIMES that she had to go to bed. And this is what Dame Edith has to say of you Jack, in her letter, and I quote her exactly: 'What a noble man Mr Cowper Powys is. His superb defence of you in the Observer was <u>magnificent</u>.'

Last night I wandered into a tavern on 86th Street, where they all spoke German and they were most friendly: a great Tom cat seemed to be in charge of the entire tavern and came and leaped up on the stool beside me and purred and talked.

I can see I will find lots to write about, if I can live through it all!

I will be interested to hear what Miss Phyllis Playter thinks of the film of MOBY DICK. I saw it not too long ago, but did not like the actor who played AHAB, as he was not nearly insane enough. But at times the picture did suggest the genius of that very great book, some of its terrible sadness and loneliness, but no film can ever bring to life a really great book, and I think MOBY DICK is that.

I will write you all the news of New York City as it happens to me. I had to buy a new pair of shoes almost at once because I am such a walker. Some times I walk all day, there is so much to see. I want to write a story about CONEY ISLAND!

I do hope you won't mind my putting your name down as a reference for a Guggenheim fellowship for next year. Let me know if this is alright. Now that I have begun to write so many stories I cannot stop.

Dame Edith is very fond of a Cuban writer named Alejo Carpentier. I read one of his books the other day El Reino de este Mundo, about Haiti, and it is splendid.[23] Several of the characters turn into animals, which the OBSERVER would find quite unnecessary, I am sure.

My dear Jack how I welcome your letters, and to know you are my loyal friend though far away over that terrible ATLANTIC. I think Dame Edith would appreciate a note from you, should you wish to write a note because she ADMIRES you greatly: her address through August is THE SES CLUB, 49 Grosvenor Street, London W.1. England.[24] I do think she would like that. Dear Jack, do write me, and God keep you strong & well, your friend, Jim

[*Powys to Purdy 24*]
Tuesday, August 20 1957

My dear Jim,

O how exciting this letter from you is! Yes I bet you are right & that you'll soon be ready to surpass [more] thrilling subjects for narrating than you have yet had. O I rejoice that you got into a Tavern where they all spoke German and there was a big Tom Cat who talked to you! You'll soon be – you <u>are</u> my dear already! – in the midst of a new Grimm's Fairy Tale <u>to be added</u> – <u>one</u> more – to that enchanting Book the <u>favourite</u> of my childhood. This walking about New York City by day is what old Dickens did about London. I love you having to get <u>new shoes</u>! <u>Hans Andersen</u> was a bit of a trial when he stayed with Dickens but <u>either</u> of the <u>Brothers Grimm</u> would have <u>got on perfectly</u> with him. I do thank you for our adored Dame's address but <u>I will be I expect too reverential towards her to write</u>. But we shall see – <u>perhaps</u> but <u>I rather doubt</u> if I'll have the guts for it! O I am so proud of Dame Edith's praise. I am so glad you told me. Phyllis was thrilled by the way the negroes played Moby Dick. They seem to have done that great work full justice. Phyllis came home from seeing it both awed and enchanted by the way they did it. She made it so real to me that I who – <u>tho' I enjoy it</u> and really falling a bit into <u>Second-childhood</u> – got for a moment the idea that all those Negroes were stopping here in Blaenau for the night!! And I asked her where they were going to put up! 'But don't you see Jack', she said 'it was a <u>Picture</u>!' They weren't actually here in Blaenau! O how I love your description, my dear Jim, of the Negress with the <u>Chicken</u>.

O I am <u>very</u> glad my dear friend that you put down my name as a reference for you to get a <u>Guggenheim Fellowship</u>,

   yrs always

<u>O Yes ! I know Coney Island</u>!!

[*Purdy to Powys 8*]
138 West 70th Street, Apt 2B, New York 23, New York
September 17, 1957

My dear Jack,
   A few days ago on a subway I saw a young lady who was reading your book UP AND OUT, and I did so want to go up to her and ask her how she liked it, and tell her I was your great admirer and correspondent for nearly a Year now! She may have been for all I know

one of the Muses! Well, that was the end of that young lady. But I have thought about her many times, sitting there in all that concourse reading your book.

That was so kind of you to allow the Guggenheim people to write you about me. Thank you, dear Jack.

Well, I have explored this old and terrible city a bit more, and have been going to a famous boxing gymnasium STILLMAN'S GYM, where all or nearly all the great boxers have trained and they allow me to sit there and hear the pugs talk.[25] I would like to write a good story about a pug. Anyhow STILLMAN'S GYM is just great, old and crumbling and like something in Jack London – who may have written about it. Then another very good place to go is ST NICHOLAS ARENA, where they still have very good boxing matches, and the talk is just wonderful, but a bit out of my price range. STILLMAN'S only costs 50 cents to listen to the pugs talk.

I wondered if you wrote our dear friend Dame Edith, but maybe she may surprise you by writing first. I believe she is in Italy, where, as you know, she lives in a Castle. (People always correct me and say You mean a Villa, but of course it is NOT a villa but a Castello or Castle, and she is in it!)

I did go to Coney Island but I was not very pleased with it after Stillman's. I think perhaps it has lost its soul. Nothing seemed quite intense enough.

Carl Van Vechten invited me to his house one afternoon and he served a drink I had never seen but had read about in a book of his (PETER WHIFFLE)[26] and this drink is called STREGA, which, as you know, means witch in Italian. I really found it quite unpleasant, but I think it does have some power of a kind, and its recipe is a secret, but I am sure it is full of FLOWERS, it is such a handsome colour. But it tastes too much like toilet water.

Did I tell you my book is to be published in GERMANY, in German translation, by a firm called Rowohlt in Hamburg. I was so astounded! And the Swedish firm Bonnier have taken out an option on it![27]

Jack how are Ajax and Diomede and Patroclus and Achilles coming?
I am rather homesick for the rolling hills of Pennsylvania.

Write me, dear friend, and I hope this finds you well and strong, and enjoying everything.

Yours, ever Jim

[*Powys to Purdy 25*]
September 20th 1957
Friday

Ye gods! I was writing Thursday forgetting which was today which was yesterday and which was tomorrow!

O no my dear Jim <u>nothing</u> would induce me to write to Dame Edith nor would I want her to write to me. Why? Simply and solely because of my overpowering admiration for her. If she wrote to me I should be simply terrified, yes! <u>Just scared</u>! I should be if I had a letter from John Cocteau or Tenassee [*sic*] Williams (I think there should be two T's in that word, but I am not good these days at spelling! It's part of my <u>Second Childhood</u>!). Or from Max Beerbohm or from Berenson both equally ideal figures of mine along with our Dame Edith. So for the sake of every god in this mad world don't'ee I beg of you suggest to her to write to me. What I venerate most I prefer to have no personal contact with!

Think of that girl in the concourse reading my book & vanishing! Let us say she was <u>Charis</u> one of the Graces who married <u>limping Hephaestus</u> the comical figure in Homer ... for any writer as old as I am Hephaestus would be the best immortal advisor – and Charis his wife would bring him from his anvils and his bellows and the twelve or twenty maidens <u>he made</u> out <u>of gold</u> and gave them enough intelligence to help his limping steps and save him from tumbling down while Charis entertained their visitors! Aye! Aye! My dear Jim, but I love what you say about <u>Stillman's Gym</u>. No I <u>never</u> knew that the Italian for witch was <u>Strega</u> – No! No! My dear friend you never told me about your being published in <u>German</u> in <u>Hamburg</u>! I do so congratulate you! I have never forgotten Hamburg where I lectured when it was a <u>Free City</u> before Prussia took it over. I used to be entertained by <u>German Jews</u>. Germans are my favourite of all races and Jews <u>come next</u> with me. And there after my lectures, they went on for about a month I fancy, and Herr Cohen who told me that all Cohens were really priests, of the

House of Levi, let me drink out of a mug given him by Hans Andersen. Personally I prefer the fairy-tales collected from country villages by the Brothers Grimm but I was proud to be so well treated aged only 22 & just down from Cambridge!

O & a Swedish firm may take it too! Hurray! Hurrah! Yes I am too old to walk for more than 20 minutes every morning before breakfast but I am astonishingly well & so is my American lady friend born in Kansas City Missouri. Do tell me for I forgot to ask him in a letter to him I've just posted how it was that Gerald Brenan read your Book? We are both great admirers of him and also very very especially of his wife who stayed with us in Corwen before their marriage. Yes I've got as far as Book XVIII of the Iliad so I am more than half way through.
Your ever affectionate old Jack.
I'm glad you've decided against Coney Island as the background of your first New York story!

[*Purdy to Powys 9*]
138 West 70th Street, Apt 2 B, New York 23, New York
October 5 1957

My dear Jack,
    I am terribly alarmed over your thinking I told Dame Edith to write to you, because NO! NO! I would not meddle like that, but dear Jack she mentioned you frequently and I think she is GOING to write to you! Please do not blame me if she does and you are TERRIFIED!
    I would not want to strain our precious friendship. But Dame Edith quoted you at great length in the LONDON TIMES LITERARY SUPPLEMENT in her review of my book and she already thinks you are a very great writer – if she writes you it is your own FATE AND DESTINY, and I am afraid you will just have to be terrified. How do you think I felt when she first wrote me from her Castle! But I was UPSET to think you would think I meddled in telling her to write you. NO! NO! Anyhow Dame Edith does always as she pleases. She told me a long time ago she admired you greatly.
    I was so interested in your liking Germans and Jews best, and I remember that in your AUTOBIOGRAPHY.

I have not yet got my copy of UP AND OUT, but I expect it momentarily now from England. I do look forward to reading it. And your HOMER!

The young girl who was reading you on the subway was undoubtedly CHARIS, which explains why she vanished and also, being Hephaestus' – why she was so close to the Bowels of the Earth. This is not a real letter but only to assure you that I did not meddle with Dame Edith to write to you. I was very upset about it, and she just wrote me from Italy and mentioned it again.

I will write very soon again a real letter, dear Jack. I am so pleased to know you are well and take those walks. There is nothing better than walking in the morning.

I saw a review of my book in THE LONDON MAGAZINE which was not quite so girlish and pious and philistine and stupid [as another review?]. The book appears in America next month, and they say there will be an outcry. This week's New York Times has an article about me. I will send it to you.

Dear Jack, please do not blame me about Dame Edith.

My sincere affection, your friend, Jim

In reply to your question about Gerald Brenan: I sent him books to his house in Spain because I admired his books very much. He wrote beautiful letters but he no longer writes, and he no longer knows where I am.

You would be interested in New York now because of the Jewish holidays. Last night I met the Spanish and Portuguese Jews coming out of their tabernacles, they had been celebrating Yom Kippur.

Tennessee Williams wrote me a long letter and asked me to meet him in New York, but I was afraid to go to see him and anyhow when he wrote I didn't have any money for such a trip and was hiding in the mountains in Pennsylvania, so I never heard from him again.

[*Powys to Purdy 26*]
October 9th 1957.

O no! No! No!
Dear friend Jim!

<u>Never never never never</u> did the idea cross my old mind that you had told me to write our <u>Grande Dame</u> <u>or</u> that you had begged her to write

to me!! Never for one second did either of those illusions cross my old mind! How dear of you to let such an idea, all erroneous as it is, worry your mind! You & I are very alike in the kind of nervous apprehensions we have. O no! I love reading everything I can about our Grande Dame but the very last thing I'd want to receive wd be a letter from her that I would have to answer.

Sun and Moon! Yes! And O I can so fully so utterly so unreservedly understand your reluctance quite apart from the question of cash of plunging into the world of or what we call it the Circle of this great Tennessee Williams. I'd be just as scared as you are of doing so! The truth is my dear Jim I begin to recognize the fact that you & I have nervous temperaments singularly alike! If anyone accused me of Homosexuality I would at once answer with the precise and exact Truth which is extremely simple; namely that in my youth it was grander to be 'Homo' than 'Hetero' – isn't it quaint to think how many people who've never been taught Greek at school but have been taught a little Latin always think that Homo means a man as it does in Latin & hetero the opposite of the same means another a different one! Such as could be called a Tart or a Bitch, or a wife. It usually does mean a bitch in Latin. But the Greek word 'hetero' means 'the other party in plural feminine Companions! other ones whereas I have only to look up these words in my Homeric Dick-John to find that the former means 'ouo or omo wh doesn't mean 'man' at all but means 'the Same' … 'omo with what we are taught to call an 'aspirate' 'c' in front of it! This 'c' is not a 'c' as it looks in my handwriting! It is a little sign 'c' in front of the 'o' telling us to pronounce this 'o' as if it were Ho!! And the same sign before the word 'etaire' turns that word into a feminine friend or companion! Yes! turns it into the word Hetaira. And so, thinking plural Heterai in my mind that it was more exciting & less committed for us to be Homo rather than Hetero, I try hard to be 'but nothing doing'! I couldn't be! So I had to submit to fate and remain Hetero!

Well I must stop. I had no less than 17 letters for my 85th birthday yesterday! So now & Phyllis joins me I pray and pray that 1958 will be a great year. It is just 4.20 p m and we have had a lovely visitor for an hour – always your old Jack.

[*Purdy to Powys 10*]
138 West 70th Street, Apt 2 B, New York 23, New York
October 14, 1957

My dear Jack,

How thrilled I was to get your splendid letter! And how relieved I am to know that you don't think I told Dame Edith to write to you. (She has a very great admiration for you, believe me, and she seldom writes me without praising your integrity and greatness!)

But how sorry I am to know only now you had a birthday. I would have sent you some little gift, and I will do so anyhow as a remembrance. Congratulations just the same on your DAY and may you see thousands of other wonderful days in Blaenau! And complete your Homer! By all means I MUST read that book. I feel it will be even greater, if that is possible, than your RABELAIS.

How really thrilling is your discussion of those words homo and hetero. I really am very queer, I suppose, in that I have NEVER believed in any of those terms. (I dont believe in words like Jew or Negro or any of them.) The main thing is to care about everybody you can, and begin where you are, and I let these words just bounce around and come out where they will. It would be a terrible world, though, with only ONE sex in it. There has to be somehow the male and the female, and nobody can be satisfied with just the one or some part of him will cry out. But I think, like you, that a life just between one sex, would be sterile and a sad one, unless maybe you were a monk, but I suspect monks are sterile and sad, at least since the time Rabelais was one! But I don't like our modern world at all, and least of all it is always pigeonholing people, dividing them up, judging, criticizing, spoiling. Nothing in nature seems so cruel.

Why cant people accept one another as they came into the world and as they are meant to be? I liked what Albert Camus said about that in La Chute: he said one does not need to wait for the Final Judgement – it happens every day. Too much judgment and not enough love.

That is what must have been so soothing about Jesus – he had no judgments to make on human beings. The awful thing about the United States, though, is that women are getting so much like men, that many men are turning to other men for their emotional satisfaction if not their emotional needs. And the men are not masculine enough for women. I think when men cease to till the soil, or be sailors or warriors or blacksmiths or hunters and just sit in offices or stores all day, they become indistinguishable in their daily activity from women, and this does begin to effect a change. Dear Jack, how I did love your letter, and that charming essay in it on the Greek language. We have been friends now almost a year! How wonderful!

My best wishes to Phyllis and congratulations and sincere affection to you. Yours ever Jim

[*Powys to Purdy 27*]
Monday October 21st 1957

No, I obey you. This is no letter. Only I just wanted to tell you that I can well understand <u>Unamuno</u> being in the atmosphere round our opening of each other's letters because Phyllis has been reading him of late & telling me a lot about his ideas. He is too religious as well as too tragic for me – I am a cheerful worshipper of many gods and goddesses but I think that when we are dead we are dead and that there is no resurrection nor any survival of our soul in any form or any shape or any existence for it when its body is dead. I believe in enjoying life while we've got it but I am sure when its gone its gone! Always – <u>till then</u>! Your old John Cowper Powys
I congratulate you on your Book being published in Spain. Yes Phyllis too is very thrilled by Spain going to publish your book: I warrant you & I have just the same reactions to Spain partly due to our devotion to Don Quixote and partly due to our hatred of the <u>Inquisition</u>.[28]

[*Purdy to Powys 11*]
138 West 70th Street, Apt 2 B, New York 23, New York
November 1, 1957

Dear Jack,
How delighted I was to hear from you about old Unamuno. I think you are right about him. You know he did not believe in God or Christ

or <u>anything</u>, not even immortality, but Christ, God and immortality were all he wanted. He was a kind of maniac.

I think I am a bit of a Greek here in that to continue as one personality forever and ever as Unamuno seemed to wish – I would find terribly boring. You would have to be God to live forever!

The greatest thing in Spain is the women, who are completely feminine and completely women, and seem to have sprung right out of the earth. They have no tricks except those of their sex. I think this is because the men are so virile still. Or maybe the men are virile because the women are so womanly.

So much human suffering is neurotically self induced today – I suppose it was even among the Greeks. But I don't believe man has to suffer as much as he does. If he could only learn to let go more! And accept what is here. Unamuno is a good example: he wanted <u>everything</u> – He wanted God.

I have lent UP AND OUT to my friends, and they are deeply impressed by it. Both stories are magnificent, each in its own way. I have ordered A GLASTONBURY ROMANCE from England. In time I shall read everything you have written.

I went to a very odd and even spooky place last Sunday. The studio of Paul Swan in Carnegie Hall. Paul Swan, it is whispered, is really a man of 80, though he appears to be quite young. Only very old people were in the audience of this small concert hall. One of the very old women said Paul Swan was 80. A gong sounded and there was a strong odor of incense. The lights were extinguished and when they came on a nearly naked man came dancing over the small stage. A rather fat woman in an evening gown announced his numbers. At the end of the program Paul Swan dressed in an oriental cap and wearing many jewels gave a long speech on individualism and the Greeks. He said he was a Greek and civilization be damned as it was today. In a way he resembled Raymond Duncan. Under all Paul Swan's strange and often outlandish behavior I felt there was a genuine man. And if he is 80 his naked dancing is certainly remarkable for its vigor if for nothing else ... I gave him my books to read. He was very much moved by them, he said, and he has invited me to tea with two of his women disciples. He is also a sculptor, as well as the leader of this strange group of mostly women. I will tell you more when I find out more.[29]

Meantime, dear Jack, I send you and Phyllis my very best wishes, and to you dear friend, my loyalty and admiration and sincere friendship. Jim
The swallowing of time by Eternity in your book is brilliant and masterful, and I will never forget it!

[*Powys to Purdy 28*]
Nov 6th 1957

O my dear how wise are your words: 'if only man could learn to let go more & accept what is here'. Aye! Jim old pal but Phyllis and your old Jack are both so impressed by your picture in words of that studio of Paul Swan in Carnegie Hall. We both agree that your words call up that best of all modern poems introduced to me when I was a youth by Thomas Hardy. I mean Edgar A. Poe's Ulalume! Yes it made me quote …

> Sit in a theatre to see
> a play of hopes and fears
> while the Orchestra breathes
> fitfully the Music of the Spheres,
> Mimes in the form of God on High
> Mutter and mumble low and
> hither and thither fly — blind
> Puppets they, that come & go
> At bidding of Vast Formless Things
> That move the Scenery to & fro
> And flap from out their Condor Wings
> Invisible woe![30]

I am so very proud, my dear, that you like Up and Out and have ordered A Glastonbury Romance, O Jim my dear & what you say about Men and Women in Spain is wonderful. I bet my life that you're right about the men being so virile because the women have no tricks but their sex and are so feminine that it is as if they sprang straight out of Gaia, the Earth or from Rhea the wife and daughter of Uranus, sister of Kronos,

Mother of Zeus, Poseidon, Hades and of Demeter and Hera – <u>Gaia</u> is always called Earth in the Iliad but Rhea is treated by <u>Ouranus</u> <u>(or as the Romans</u> called Him <u>Uranus</u>) <u>as if she were his</u> wife and Kronos is treated as the first son of Rhea who was <u>not</u> a monster or a Titan. Kronos the first human-like son of Rhea cut out the balls of his father Uranus with a knife made of jagged flint which his mother Rhea gave him to do it with as she was tired of giving birth to Titans and Monsters whom Ouranus or Uranus never ceased to beget upon her!

O I shall work my magic as an Enchanter to fill the sails of your imagination as you work on your new book and you must send whirling & hurling thro' the air your blessing on my Iliad book. Which is a <u>paraphrase not</u> a translation. <u>Always your old Jack</u>

[*Purdy to Powys 12*]
138 West 70th Street, Apartment 2, New York 23, New York
December 7, 1957

Dear Jack,
    A GLASTONBURY ROMANCE arrived, the new edition, with your new Preface, and I am completely engrossed in it. I have already read 300 and some pages. What wonderful and deep portraits of human beings! (I like to go slow with it so that it will last longer.) The insight into women (and men) is so great, as on pages 298-299.[31] I do love the MAGIC IN YOUR books – magic of every kind and description. I am very much moved by it, I can tell you!

    I hope this letter finds you and Phyllis well and all well in Blaenau.

    My book has now been <u>conventionally</u> and <u>formally</u> published in the USA.[32] It received a good review in TIME magazine, – the leading review of the book section. The book was officially published December 4 – if books are <u>officially</u> published.

    I have found out through my short period as an author that people are both finer and viler than I ever dreamed.

    Dame Edith is coming to America in March, and she says she will certainly see me and Victor Gollancz is coming in January, and he will see me also … Now, Jack, you and Phyllis should come also!

I have been spending an awful lot of time in the Central Park Zoo, and am having silent conversations with the younger gorillas, who are interested in my buttons and hat, and also the sacks of groceries I carry. The coati is one of my favourite animals, too; do you know him, from South America ... I came upon a scene behind the Camel house. A woman no longer young but wearing gaily-colored shawls and a great blue hat was kissing passionately one of the guards near the Camel House. They did not see me, but after the woman had left the embraces of the guard (he promised to see her at closing time) and when she had got her breath again, she went inside the Camel house. I followed her in there to see what great thing she would do next. She went up immediately to the largest of the bactrian camels, caressed his hair, and then fed him some gum-drops which she had carried expressly (evidently) for the beast. A very odd and doubtless powerful woman, subduing both men and beasts – though I doubt she would win over the gorillas.

Do write me the news, and please tell me if the place-name BLAENAU may have a meaning ... I am so pleased, I must repeat, to have A GLASTONBURY ROMANCE. With every good wish, dear Jack, and regards to Phyllis, Sincere friendship, your pal, Jim

[*Powys to Purdy 29*]
Tuesday Dec 10 1957

Let me answer quickly before I forget my dear Jim your last question about Blaenau. Yes the Roman General Festinus – the Welsh have to put two FFs if they want the word to sound like our F. One Welsh F sounds like our v yes like v this general who gave his name to Ffestiniog when the Romans were invading Britain soon after Caesar's attempt – I think these must have been associated in all the minds of the Roman legionaries under his command with the Latin motto Festine Lente which literally means quickly slowly and as general rather like our 'Monty' he must in his tactics and strategy have combined quick decisions with cautious planning. Well he had got his legion (if it was as large a body of troops as that) to a large well-constructed eminence which is now our Ffestiniog or as we local dwellers call it (leaving out Blaenau) Llan-Festiniog or just simply Llan, a word that means a district, a yard or a church. The Roman General hesitated at this point. He was looking for some spot that would be a perfect site for a firmly established Roman Camp such as could last some time. As he hesitated whether to select as his 'Llan' the hill he had just reached he enquired of some British Welsh natives and they all cried 'O blaen! O blaen' (in English blaen wd be pronounced bline) which means in Welsh 'on! on!' So he ordered his legions to march on. And so they came to Blaenau which is a village built not like 'Llan' on a rounded hill but on a ridge overlooking the wide valley which extending East [West] straight down to Port Madoc from which the (wild) Welsh or British (if we should call the Welsh British) – as we ought to do – they were divided in those days into many separate tribes. All this is told in the Mabinogion – into English by Lady Charlotte Guest in 1847 and quite recently by two Welsh Professors of the Welsh University of Aberystwyth about 50 miles from here: one of which I stayed with and he came to visit me later bringing with him an Icelandic Professor when my American lady Miss Playter and I lived at Corwen. Yes the Mabinogion is the story of the pre-historic time of Wales long before Danes or Saxons appeared at all!

Our most exciting news is that my New York sister the Lace Lady will visit us in March. She is now with my only surviving brother Wm E. Powys in Kenya Africa.

We are both so glad to possess your book officially published and I love to think of Dame Edith seeing you in March and Gollancz in January. I am so proud and so pleased my dear Jim that you like my Glastonbury Book. Yrs always, JC Powys

The only book equal to yours is a recent French novel called Double Exposure by Theo Fleischmann now translated into English.[33]

1958   Powys to Purdy 30-38
Purdy to Powys 13-16

[*Powys to Purdy 30*]
The First Night of 1958

O I do so thank you my dear Jim for sending me the new proper official thoroughly Americanized Copy of your now world-famous

Book![34] You can imagine old as I am what a whirl of struggles to save my perishing memory I have been plunged in between Xmas and New Year letters! However this little tiny envelope which I have been keeping carefully in my pocket has now fulfilled & perfected its task to remind me to thank you a thousand times my dear Jim for this Book. O <u>How</u> nice it looks in its new form! How proud of itself and its author! Well my friend good luck in your <u>New Work</u> always your old Jack & so says Mr. Jack's Phyllis.

[*Powys to Purdy 31*]
January the 8th 1958
My dear Jim

    I am so pleased you met those two men Norman Notley and David Brynley.[35] O you are <u>so wise</u> my dear Jim to stay in that <u>unfashionable</u> part of town with Negroes and Puerto Ricans etc etc. I have been too overwhelmed with answering letters to give the time I am so longing to give to my Homeric Book – this letter answering is the Devil! Have you noticed my dear Jim the peculiarity of the Xmas and New Year cards this season? They have deserted 'Our Lady' & poor old Joseph sits sulking [in] both the Inn and the shed! But they now concentrate on little Cherubs with wings! Before long they'll be giving little baby Jesus a pair of wings – and off he'll fly escaping to fairy land to avoid the burden of having to become the second Person of the Trinity. The other peculiarity I've noticed in the Xmas cards of this year pleases me, more than the cherubs! That is the number of excellent cards, bigger than the cherub ones, with <u>Books</u> and <u>Candles</u> – I've had about four of these & felt almost reluctant to take them down from chimney-piece and book[shelf]. And I've had for quite a long time – I don't know how many years – a lovely picture that might have been the origin of all these Xmas <u>Book and Candles</u> pictures.

    It is by a painter called <u>Gerard Dow</u>[36] and it is a picture of the Mother of Rembrandt reading a big book and holding it so close to her eyes! Someone ought to write a book – a sort of psychological <u>history book</u> – upon Xmas Cards – showing how since they began – I have no idea when that was! up to the present year, they have expressed the character of the age, or of the particular <u>year</u> when they were made [&] sold.

Well you 'pray' – by 'pray' I mean <u>will</u> – and send by your will every vibration over the sea that I shall be able to write a good <u>preface</u> to my Homer book and I'll 'pray', I mean <u>will</u> that your present <u>work</u> turns out a masterpiece greater than anything yet.   yours always

[*Powys to Purdy 32*]
Monday, Feb 3 1958

My dear Jim
   O I do so love your description of that tiny little <u>Fly</u> at the <u>South Pole</u>. <u>O yes</u>! <u>Yes</u>! <u>This information from you about this little Fly at the South Pole</u> delights me. Aye! My dear & I do rejoice at your meeting with our great Gollanzc – I <u>always forget which letter comes first & which comes last</u> – <u>and I pray indeed to Pallas Athene that he will accept Malcolm</u>. Aye! My dear <u>dear</u> Jim, my <u>only</u> Jim! I had no expectation that you had got so far with it as to have a Rough Draft of it to let your publisher read! No I had no idea you were more than just <u>slowly beginning beginning</u> it! And I am so proud of you that you have actually had <u>offers from Russia</u> about which you have told them to consult with David Higham of Pearn, <u>Pollinger and Higham</u> of Dean St. Soho London and Hurrah! Hurrah! Hurrah! The publishers of Prague and of Denmark, Japan, Italy, Norway, Sweden, Spain & Portugal!!! O my dear dear Jim I am so grateful to you for getting all sorts and conditions of people to read Up and Out. I do hope I shall be able to think up a group of original enough people mothers fathers uncles aunts young men & maidens and children however odd and crazy they may be to write my new human fairy tale for my way of story-telling, Jim old friend, is to let the characters themselves whether they are rocks or stones or trees or cats or dogs or people <u>use my pen</u> (which has got a very special <u>nib</u> made of gold) to tell the stories one after the other taking up the tale. O I do indeed hope '<u>Malcolm</u>' will prove a grand success. I think it is really wonderful that you have finished it so soon. Your example encourages me to work hard at my new tale which so far is only collecting itself together as you might say to make a start – the gods guard you & Malcolm – always.
   Your old Jack

[*Purdy to Powys 13*]
February 23 1958

Dear dear Jack,
 I am always so thrilled when you tell me that you will send those 'winged thoughts' to me across that great expanse of Ocean – because, Jack, I do oh so certainly feel them. and I do try to send strong hopeful creative ones back to you – and I do believe they must reach you – I have been doing a lot of silent kind of meditation and prayer, and God knows I need it – who doesn't – because I have promised Miss Lilian Hellman who wrote 'The Little Foxes' and 'The Children's Hour' – that I will try my hand at writing a play for Broadway! After I told her I would do it, I was HORRIFIED at what I had promised – almost as horrified as if I had told her I would erect a new skyscraper with my own two hands! Well, the fat is in the fire and I am writing a play called MADONNA, together with my novel MALCOLM …. MADONNA has to do with a possessive kind of mother, a kind of sacred WHORE type, who has had so many lovers she actually DOES NOT remember who is the father of her son, 15 years old; he is passionately concerned with finding out who his father is, and the MADONNA is just as passionately lost in the remembrance or non-remembrance of her past lovers, all of whom could have been fit to have been, she feels, the Father of Anybody.
 That must sound terribly stupid!
 I should not tell you this, and yet why not, since we send winged thoughts to one another, but NEW DIRECTIONS are very much desirous of republishing one of your great long novels here in the United States, and I told them how great A GLASTONBURY ROMANCE was, and how I had fallen in love with all those characters, especially Mr. Geard, Sam Dekker, and Nell Zoyland. Then NEW DIRECTIONS said that your name had been proposed for the NOBEL PRIZE by a very great British woman of letters, and I am not to tell you this, or they will be very cross, but I am sure you know it anyhow, and I am feeling the NOBEL PRIZE will be yours Jack, – if you want it, that is, I feel it will, but if anything, it is not good enough for you, for you are better than almost anybody who ever won it. I hope you will not be cross for my whispering these things into your ear – but I was very much thrilled

that this great British lady whom you admire so much had placed your name before the Committee.

Last night some very wealthy people took me out to dinner and then to Eugene O'Neill's grand play LONG DAY'S JOURNEY INTO NIGHT, which is a staggering four-hour tragedy, and I have not recovered from it yet.

I was very saddened to learn from our Dame Edith that she is not coming to America after all; she has had some kind of to-do with her manager here in the USA and she says she will not come this year, which is a terrible disappointment to me, so she has gone back to London, as has Victor Gollancz.

I saw a rather fair movie based on the autobiography of Frank Harris, who always did interest me – this was his cowboy career in the United States, and I don't know whether he told the truth about any of that or not, but it made a fair film.[37]

I read rather alarming things about the weather in North Wales, and I hope you were not snowbound. We had so many inches of snow here, this immense old filthy metropolis was paralyzed, at least from the waist down, and she could only lie there for a day or so and roar. I am quite frightened sometimes of New York when I think of all that twisted metal, wires, cables, miles of steel overhead, the whirling milling machinery of the whole thing where ever you turn; how does it manage not blowing up of itself. Anyhow, the snow got it and held it for a day.

I have decided that the colored man who cleans my windows for me smells like a butterfly when it has struck against something heavy and lost some of its pollen; anyhow that has been an odor that always puzzled me, the smell of Negroes when they are working. There is a fine passage on it in Faulkner's Intruder in the Dust, but after smelling it all day I decided it was butterfly in essence. The Negroes say we smell awful to them. But we cant know really how we smell because we are white!

I'm afraid this is an idiotic letter – it is because I have been cooped up for a week with all this snow. Now I can get out and go walking again.

Dear Jack, I send you my very best thoughts and wishes, and every affectionate greeting to you, and to Phyllis my very best wishes. Your friend, Jim

[Powys to Purdy 33]
February 27th 1958

My dear Jim

   Well! You are a one! Just think of you having the courage to write a play for Broadway! I would be scared stiff in your shoes. But you are nothing if not an incorrigible and unterrifyable genius, my dear Jim! I admire you and look at your activity with a sort of awe – I am at this moment reading the life of Jules Verne by Marguerite Allotte de la Fuy.[38] There's a grand name for you! Her biography of this French writer translated into English by Eric de Mauny and published by Staples Press at London is very lively and amusing but a bit too feminine in tone for a particular and critical old gent like your Jack. But it was in English translation that when I was a boy I simply worshipped Jules Verne! He was then and in many ways still is my favourite of all writers of exciting stories. 'Thirty Thousand Leagues under the sea' 'Round the world in eighty days' O how they thrilled me – Even yet, my dear Jim, whenever I see the sun go down round & red I say to myself à la Captain Nemo: Descend thou radiant Orb. That story of your play Madonna certainly does sound extremely good O I do pray it will make a great hit. It may you know. It very likely will! – O I am so glad to hear about it. Well! I've actually found the English First Edition of my book Wolf Solent which I am [giving] as a present to a collector of my family's books in Williamstown College Williamstown Pa. who is collecting all books he can get by us Powyses. He is a young assistant librarian at the Chapin Library in his College.[39] Well I am now beginning a new story of my very own.

   I have nearly finished helping Phyllis to correct the typescript of my Book on Homer's Iliad which we shall shortly be sending to my publisher. The next book of mine to appear in print will be a Book of letters to my friend Louis M Wilkinson alias Louis Marlow. I do love what you say my dear Jim about the sweat of negroes smelling like Butterflies.

   I think the plot of Madonna sounds splendid – and I am longing to read Malcolm. What a man you are! All the gods be with you. Always your old Jack Powys.

[*Powys to Purdy 34*]
March 3 1958

My dear Jim

    I do congratulate you from my heart for all these grand Tributes from all our best Moderns on the Color of Darkness published by <u>New Directions</u>. I am <u>especially pleased</u> by what William Carlos Williams says. I <u>am so glad, my dear Jim, that you sent me these Tributes. I have got, and so has my American Lady, intense satisfaction</u> from them.

    Don't 'ee hurry, my dear dear friend, about writing to me till a calm peace supervenes and Malcolm is rounded off a la your best ideal … Well! Our mutual idol the great Dame E. was justified in her attitude to your work! It was the work of our friend Henry Miller that first introduced me to the words 'NEW DIRECTIONS'. Those words sank into my old-fashioned pate, which in its old-fashioned second childhood is still recalling such things as the insulting & extremely Scotch & insolent comments of Thomas Carlisle upon Charles Lamb and his Mentally Afflicted Sister Mary Lamb and which is still dedicating all its best imperatives to the womb from which it came namely that of Mary Cowper Powys née Cowper Johnson – of Norfolk & of the city which the Man in the Moon too soon asked his way namely Norwich.[40] Don't 'ee hurry my dear Jim about anything   yr old Jack.

[*Purdy to Powys 14*]
138 West 70th Street, Apartment 2 B, New York 23, New York, United States
March 29, 1958

My dear Jack,

    I was so delighted to hear about the new volume of yours which contains your correspondence:[41] I had tried to get this at the British Book Center, but they didn't have it at the time, and I got your <u>Rabelais</u> instead, which is so brilliant. I have a beautiful little Urquhart translation of him.

    But the thing which is the most thrilling is that you have finished your <u>Homer</u>! I can't tell you how eager I am to get that and read it!

My head is swimming, as they are putting pressure on me to finish my play, which is called Madonna, and then I have to entirely rewrite, and change, my novel Malcolm. I am just as frightened about writing a play for Broadway as anybody could be but the only things I seem to be able to do are the impossible things! I never could do any of the things that seemed the possible things. But If I don't try the impossible things, my life comes to an end.

Recently I studied in the Bronx zoo, a strange white hedgehog, from some far off place, Tibet or some such region, I believe, and the parasol Ants, which carry large petals of flowers over their heads, so that they look like ladies on the way to church.

How very interesting that it was Henry Miller who introduced you to New Directions. Alfred Knopf wanted to publish Color of Darkness also but somehow, my agent told me, New Directions outbid them.

A very odd thing is now going on: the movies are interested in making a film of 63: DREAM PALACE, I cannot believe this! But a famous Hollywood director talked to me a very little bit about it, asking little queer questions here and there of me. I was too astonished to say much to him. They are studying the problem, as they say.

Spring has come enough for one to allow his windows to be open, but there isn't a sign of a robin – at least two weeks late!

I am very pleased with the photograph of you on the back of your Rabelais.

One question I have been meaning to ask you: is the EVERYMAN edition of Malory's Morte D'Arthur a satisfactory and complete text. I have seen some very expensive texts that are most beautiful, but I wondered if Everyman was complete and authentic. I do want to read all of Malory.

I do hope this letter finds you and Phyllis in the best of health and enjoying spring weather. Oh, how tired I am of winter. Every good wish to you, and again how delighted I am that Homer is ready for publication; I am really so thrilled to look forward to this. Affectionate best wishes to you and Phyllis from your friend, Jim

P.S. I can't get interested in these literary people in New York, and I have abandoned them completely, except Carl Van Vechten, who is at heart a rogue.

CORRESPONDENCE

[*Powys to Purdy 35*]
Wednesday, April 2 1958

My dear Jim

O no! those Letters of mine aren't published yet! But they will be soon. But they are all to <u>one person</u> & I guess that detracts a little, don't you think? from their interest? O but I am so glad you found my Rabelais. I worked hard at that book with the help of <u>Littré's</u> French-French dictionary, a huge work – a sort of <u>French Johnson's Dictionary</u>! I hear they put my Rabelais along with other books on the greatest of men whom <u>Shakespeare</u> quotes when he says or someone in his plays says he'd need <u>the mouth of Gargantua</u> in the Rabelais museum in his home village of <u>Mendon</u> [for Chinon]on the little river Vienne. How extraordinarily exciting my dear Jim that you've had a visit from <u>Hollywood</u> about making a <u>Film</u> of that <u>Dream Palace</u> book! I don't wonder you feel a bit scared. But that does explain, my dear Jim, your inmost soul, when you talk of your mania for the <u>Impossible</u>. You'll do it! You'll make it! Yes I expect the <u>Everyman</u> edition of <u>Malory</u> is O.K. We've the great big Malory in 2 big volumes and you talking of it set me off reading <u>Caxton's Preface</u> to it – think of your first great <u>Printer printing</u> that Book! His Preface to it is so practical & so sensible and so good. But that <u>Everyman</u> editor is safe to follow. I would trust those people know what they are doing. I don't like hearing that you are going to <u>rewrite</u> your novel called <u>Malcolm</u>. You beat me there. I never <u>have</u> & never <u>could</u> <u>rewrite</u> a novel. Well! Jim dear, good luck to facing all these excitements and agitations! O yes today the sky was <u>absolutely blue</u> all over! Not even a white cloud! Yr Jack yrs always J C Powys

[*Purdy to Powys 15*]
138 West 70th Street, Apartment 2 B, New York 23, New York USA
June 20th, 1958

Dear Jack

A colored woman who works in a butcher shop gave me some lamb fries (lamb testicles) to 'cook for myself' for supper, and I had to take them home, but the sight of them has made me quite sick, and I have even thought I may never taste <u>meat again</u>. The thought of cutting off the testicles of so <u>small</u> a beast is also quite shocking – even though these look quite large I will let them stay over night and tomorrow when the Italian janitor comes I will give them to <u>him</u>. Anyhow, these lamb testicles have completely changed the tenor of my day, and I may not be myself for several days. I feel I have witnessed some strange carnage.

I am studying ancient Greek with a young Greek man from the Greek Orthodox Cathedral, who has, it seems to me, a very un-Greek name: Jacques Case and I must find out from him how on earth he got this name. I am still writing that play, and the producers are not very pleased with what I have done, but they are sure, they say, that I can do it. I am getting mad at the whole thing. I may sit down and write something perfectly outrageous. Those testicles may be my inspiration to DEMOLISH the theater.

I also have that hideous novel MALCOLM awaiting revisions which you, dear, say not to do. My publisher, James Laughlin, said MALCOLM gave him nightmares for three nights after he read it. But I never think of myself as a horror writer. It is about a really pleasant boy of 14.

Dame Edith has written again a very nice letter from her stay at the Sesame Club in London. And so has Victor Gollancz. The weather, I am sure, is changing owing to all these bombs and fumes from industrial civilization.

I went to quite a nice exhibition of Carl Van Vechten's photographs of the Negro – at the Museum of the City of New York – covering a period of nearly thirty years. All the great American Negroes had been photographed by him and all their faces watching you from the walls were quite impressive.

I must watch myself or when I get the Guggenheim money I will turn into a very lazy no-account person!

Do you know the Ozarks – the mountains – I am sure you know them because you were everywhere in the United States. My play is <u>slightly</u> about that country but it is the Ozarks I think about when I write the play. I am very fond of the Shenandoah Valley also. There are so many parts of the United States which are mysterious and rather lost, and which have not yet been captured by this civilization. I think it was Emerson who said that he had the feeling when he rode by that the <u>trees</u> were waiting for him to leave, so that they could resume their life. I have this feeling about certain parts of the United States: they are waiting for us to leave. Dear Jack, I think of you so often, and hope you are well and strong and happy.

My best regards to Phyllis, and my very best to you, dear friend, Jim I have got hold of the Kalevala, which is a nice companion to The Mabinogion, but I think the Mabinogion is much stranger than the Kalevala.[42]

[*Powys to Purdy 36*]
Tuesday October 28 1958

My dear Jim

I was so pleased to get this letter from you O my unique old friend I <u>have been</u> and <u>am</u> and <u>shall</u> be on the wind round you praying for you in Saturnalian days and Elysian days and Plutonian days not to speak of the days when Demeter appears at every cross road and at every milestone, waiting, waiting, in hope of getting her daughter back, yes yes yes yes indeed! There is no poetic or dramatic creation to touch Goethe in that great motto of his 'im ganzen guten schoenen resolut zu leben' 'live in the whole, the good and the true [*sic*]' he <u>doesn't</u> say 'live in the <u>Truth</u>' because he knows that all bigoted narrow & fanatic people want you to live in <u>Truth</u> as they call it! <u>Their</u> bloody truth, <u>their</u> confounded idea of truth! He says 'im ganzen' 'in the <u>whole</u>' yes <u>in the whole bloody business</u>! 'In the universe – in the cosmic' ' in the universe or the multiverse'!

O my dear I do pray pray pray pray that <u>Malcolm</u> <u>will</u> be a terrific success. My <u>Phyllis</u> was so pleased you didn't forget her – yes I saw in our papers that Dame Edith had a great ovation. Now I am waiting for tomorrow's paper to read about the NEW POPE. They say he's an Italian. Well! <u>That's</u> right. That's as it should be.

Your devoted Old Jack

[*Powys to Purdy 37*]
Monday November 17 1958

My dear Jim
　O how pleased I am that you agree with me about Poe. It was none other than Thomas Hardy who was the first to introduce me to his poetry. But I had read his tales in my boyhood just as I read in those early days English translations of Jules Verne who has recently and quite justly had such a lively revival. I am so interested to hear of your new Publisher for your Malcolm; and I'm glad New Directions has forgiven you & released you.[43] O yes my old friend I am one with you entirely about the new pope. Like you I am not a Christian but like you I have a mania for Jesus as a real historic great and I had a picture of the dead Pope (whom I still think was one of the greatest of them all and I wish they would canonize him) but I destroyed it from among my most precious pictures and photos when I found he had let that nice old nun who looked after him till he died persuade him to take a medicine that had been discovered by Vivisection. Both Phyllis and I are fanatical Anti-vivisectionists. Anti-vivisection is indeed at the bottom of both our hearts our one and only Cause. O my dear Jim how I do share your feeling about Eckermann's Conversations with Goethe. I didn't know that Nietzsche said it was the Greatest Book in German. Aye! But I'm glad he said that. I shall never forget when my cousin Alice Shirley took me to Nietzsche's house soon after his death to have tea with his sister Frau Forster Nietzsche and how interested I was in his Books especially when I found they were almost all French Books! With O such exciting comments by Nietzsche in the margins of them.
　Well my dearest Jim good luck to your work, it'll live – I know that much about it! – long long after we are all dead. yrs always & always. Jack

[*Powys to Purdy 38*]
Tuesday, Dec 16th 1958

　Aye Jim old friend I am so interested in this letter of yours posted on the 12th and here it is on the 16th – just 4 days! I rejoice in having you as a companion of my lady and me as a crusader against vivisection.

I love your word from the Zoo keeper as to the healthy smell of horses' and cattle Dung compared with the horrid stink of human turds! And think of your making friends with that Gorilla and seeing that lowest form of monkey called by a name that sounds like 'Galago'.

But Oh! My dear Jim the real great news is that you have finished or <u>are in the act of finishing Malcolm</u>. Hurrah! And Oh! I am so glad that your new Publishers say that they <u>will</u> take it and as you put it ascend the <u>gallows</u> with you!

[Picture of gallows here]

Aye! My dear Jim and I am so glad you like my letters to Louis Wilkinson. That book <u>seems</u> to be selling just now better that any of my other books. Louis W's mother was my mother's best friend and my brother Theodore went to Wilkinson's Father's school at Aldeburgh in Suffolk when Theodore was 14 and Louis was 8. My Publisher, the Boss of Macdonald's, hopes to publish my 'Homer and the Aether' in January. I do pray I'll have corrected the Proofs etc. in time for that. I've just finished another Story of the sort that people these days call a '<u>Space Travel Book</u>' entitled <u>All or Nothing</u> but <u>that</u> will have to wait a bit before it comes out. With real affection my dear Jim & good luck to <u>Malcolm</u> & so says my Phyllis, always your old Jack.

[*Purdy to Powys 16*]
December 1958

For Jack and Phyllis

Christmas greetings for 1958 – May this Christmas and New Year be a most happy one and rich for you both.

Jack I did <u>love</u> your last letter and will reply very soon – your letters <u>electrify</u> my whole week. I love your new book of letters from John Bumpus bookstore. Wonderful! I have also been reading Lord Byron's Collected Letters and so do admire them and him.

Every good wish to you both.

Your ever and ever Jim

Your handwriting is that of a strong man of 25!

1959 Powys to Purdy 39-51
   Purdy to Powys 17-18
   Powys to Lynn Caine

[*Powys to Purdy 39*]
Friday, February 6th 1959

My dear Jim

   Hurrah for that Farrar, Straus, and Cudahy are publishing your MALCOLM! And doing so – aye <u>that is</u> the important point just as you have written it. O my dear I'm longing to read it so please please please send a copy & I will read it aloud all through <u>every evening</u> to my Phyllis until we have finished it! I shall be as excited over the Publication of a Book of mine soon on Feb 27th – published by Macdonald & Company 16 Maddox St London <u>Homer and the Aether</u>. It is a translation word for word of the Iliad with a running commentary from beginning to end by a Goddess I have invented called <u>the Aether</u>. She gives <u>thoughts</u> of all other characters while Homer gives their <u>actions</u>. I am <u>so</u> thrilled my dear Jim at your pleasure in my Letters to Louis: His [mother] was my mother's greatest friend and my brother Theodore went to his Father's School for boys at Aldeburgh in Suffolk. He wrote a book long ago about us all called <u>Welsh Ambassadors</u> describing his visit to Montacute in Somerset where the last three of us eleven children were born. Five of us were born in Shirley Vicarage Derbyshire three of us in Dorchester in Dorsetshire and the last three in Montacute Somerset. There are now only two boys left alive, John the eldest of the eleven and William a Farmer in Kenya East Africa and only three girls Marian in America and Katie (or Philippa) and Lucy the youngest of us in Dorset.
   I love to think of your sending a Valentine to Dame Edith in her castle in Florence – we are both wonderfully well considering the snow the frost and the ice! But the rain yes has come to our rescue!
   Love from us both my dear & we are both longing to read '<u>Malcolm</u>'

[*Powys to Purdy 40*]
Monday March 2nd 1959

My dear Jim,
 I am so very interested by this change in your address. I am so proud and delighted that your friend has already ordered my <u>Homer and the Aether</u>. What a good choice you made my dear Jim in settling in Brooklyn near the Sea. Aye! How well you do put it Jim! That you <u>now can imagine Hell</u> quite all right. But you want to see the SEA! Yes I am indeed longing to read your <u>Malcolm</u>. I should <u>read it aloud to Phyllis</u> every evening till I've got to the end. I like your good word for Carl Van Vechten and I agree with it. Think of your living in the house of an old dead sea-captain! Aye! But I am O so impatient to be reading Malcolm aloud to Phyllis in her Parlour downstairs which is where we sleep at night. I say 'downstairs' but this is a tiny half-house and these 'stairs' are only 9 <u>steps</u>. I am a great lover of <u>invention</u> I love inventing <u>characters</u> and in reality when once I've invented them I leave <u>whatever</u> tale I am writing <u>to them</u> and they can go on and finish it as they like. I dont write my books. My characters write them. But O I so love inventing weird strange horrible devilish saintly funny mischievous puckish mysterious characters! And then I leave the tale to them. I've already finished (after the Homer was done) <u>another story</u> of my own called '<u>All or Nothing</u>' and I have now begun one called '<u>You and Me</u>'. But perhaps my excellent publishers will not want to publish these crazy books! We shall see. Anyway I've enjoyed writing them! Ever your old Jack.

[*Powys to Purdy 41*]
March 14 1959

My dear Jim
 O yes I bet <u>it is</u> the Sea and Walt and Melville that between them stirred you up and inspired you to write 'NEPHEWS'. Heavens! old friend Jim. But I love to hear of this Book – the idea of it delights me. I am exactly in the same position as your old People's brother & sister. I have such exciting nephews (& nieces too) and I've got one sister in

New York and two in Dorset one of whom set out on the 12th – the day before yesterday (Friday 13th) which would hardly have been a good day to start for anywhere! Yes I love the thought of what you call this book's 'sappy gaiety'! And I am glad you make DEATH not so terribly terrible – for that is my own attitude to it! Think of you being able dear Jim to see the Statue of Liberty from your room. O I am so thankful you have made this move. It'll do you good & through you it'll do your readers good! All the same for that as Homer makes Achilles reply to his horse when the horse warns him he's going to die 'all the same for that'. I do wish Malcolm great good luck   yours ever and always Jack

[*Powys to Purdy 42*]
Friday April 17th 1959

Dear Jim
   O yes! You have got your Impressions that's what your letters are: living flying walking swimming through the walls and waters and fires and airs by this crazy atom-filled Space which surmounts us! A giant's impressions a Siren's impressions a Faun's impressions, a Satyr's impressions or Pan's impressions, a Bacchus's Impressions O my dear old Jim I do from my heart congratulate you on this memorable visit from Signore Giangiacomo Feltrinelli about publishing MALCOLM in Italian![44] I am glad you heard from Dame Edith. Her blessing on your labours will be I am certain like [the] blessing of Hera upon Hercules. But I [was] shocked to hear of her brother having Parkinson's Disease.[45] O I pray they'll deal with that awful thing successfully. Just had a letter from such a quaintly named lady in Washington D.C. Her name is a beautiful name, a mischievously playful name, a Queen of Ballerina's name, a swaying sea-bird's name! I wonder what she is like and whether [she] is quite as lovely and alluring as her name. Her name is Adeline Frixielle.
   Well my dear Jim, you ask me if it's Spring in Blaenau. Well! The only flowers I've yet seen are a pair of Dandelions. And only blossoms I've seen yet White blossoms of the Blackthorn. The Hawthorn is only just in leaf; but there is a lovely white blackthorn bush where I walk every

morn before breakfast for a quarter of an hour beneath a tremendous waterfall which the recent rains have turned into a grand rush of water. I am often meeting a Black Slug which I carry to a Magic Stone and then lay him down in the grass round near the Stone –

[sketch]

I have 4 sticks each with a separate name 'Sherborne', 'Saviour', 'Cheiron', 'Together' and the last day of the month I have an enormously big stick called EXPECTATION and for the first day of the month a very little stick made of African Ebony called Hoo-Doo. Today I started holding SHERBORNE but the rain drove me back.

During the whole day I lie on my back on a couch at my window writing my books and looking on at the mountains. I can see Two Peaks one called Moelwyn Bach and the other called Moelwyn Mawr. The first means little White mountain and the second means the Big (White) Mountain

[Ink sketch]

Yes I take that excellent Jewish magazine you speak of[46] and read ENCORE with great delight – I [like] it very much indeed.[47] I was so excited to find a story of yours in that magazine. So now I've got two copies of it & can send one to a friend. My Publisher is now reading a Book I've written after the Homer one entitled 'ALL OR NOTHING' – I do hope he will like it well enough to publish it. It's about a group of people flying into space and carrying earth-mould beyond the Milky Way to make a new star. Well I must stop it is ten p.m. Bed-time for me! Yrs ever & always. J C Powys.

[*Powys to Purdy 43*]
Saturday, June 20th 1959

Dear Jim

I am so thrilled you enjoyed my Homer and the Aether. O I am so longing to get a copy of Malcolm & I am so glad Dame Edith liked it. I love her saying her humour is half American & half British! Last night on our BBC there was somebody questioning [her] & O how honest and direct all her answers were! She is a one! I prefer her to her two almost equally famous brothers Osbert and Sacheverel. I am so very interested, my dear Jim, to hear that you have actually finished the first draft of your new Novel entitled THE NEPHEW! I sure do my dear send you a special charm from all six magic sticks – from Sherborne, Saviour, Cheiron, Together, Expectation, & Hoo-Doo. I pray that in combination with one unseen platform I no longer use they will make the Nephew a great success.

I have been reading Chaucer in the Everyman Library where he is perfectly interpreted and explained.

Think of Carl Van Vechten 80 on the 18th of this month! O my dear Jim but I'm thrilled your first Book has appeared in German especially in Hamburg and is praised in DIE WELT. How interesting that you & I should both be appreciated so much in Germany! It was recently from the Hamburg Society of Fine Arts that Rolf Italiaander their Secretary brought me & presented to me here in Blaenau a Bronze Plaque with my name engraved on it along with the Heraldic Three Harbours of Hamburg. The city where I lectured on Shakespeare in English for I only know one line of German, Goethe's 'im ganzen, Guten, Schoenen, resolut zu leben' 'Resolve to live in the whole, in the Good, in the Beautiful' which means in the whole universe instead of in the Truth which means in my special view of things.

I love to hear my dear Jim of that store on Vesey Street 114 years old you've found which sells double yolk Duck eggs and Blueberry cakes! Think of the Staten Island Ferry only costing a nickel! Think of your seeing Raymond Duncan in his Greek costume. I bet he didn't look more daring than Harry Truman whom I admire very very very very much!

I used to always carry about with me a little edition of Walt Whitman published by Routledge. He is the favourite of all writers to my sister Katie Philippa Powys who is the poetess of our family of eleven children.

Our Blaenau sheep & lambs are far more spirited than the Dorset ones I used to see in my youth.

Yours ever, Jack

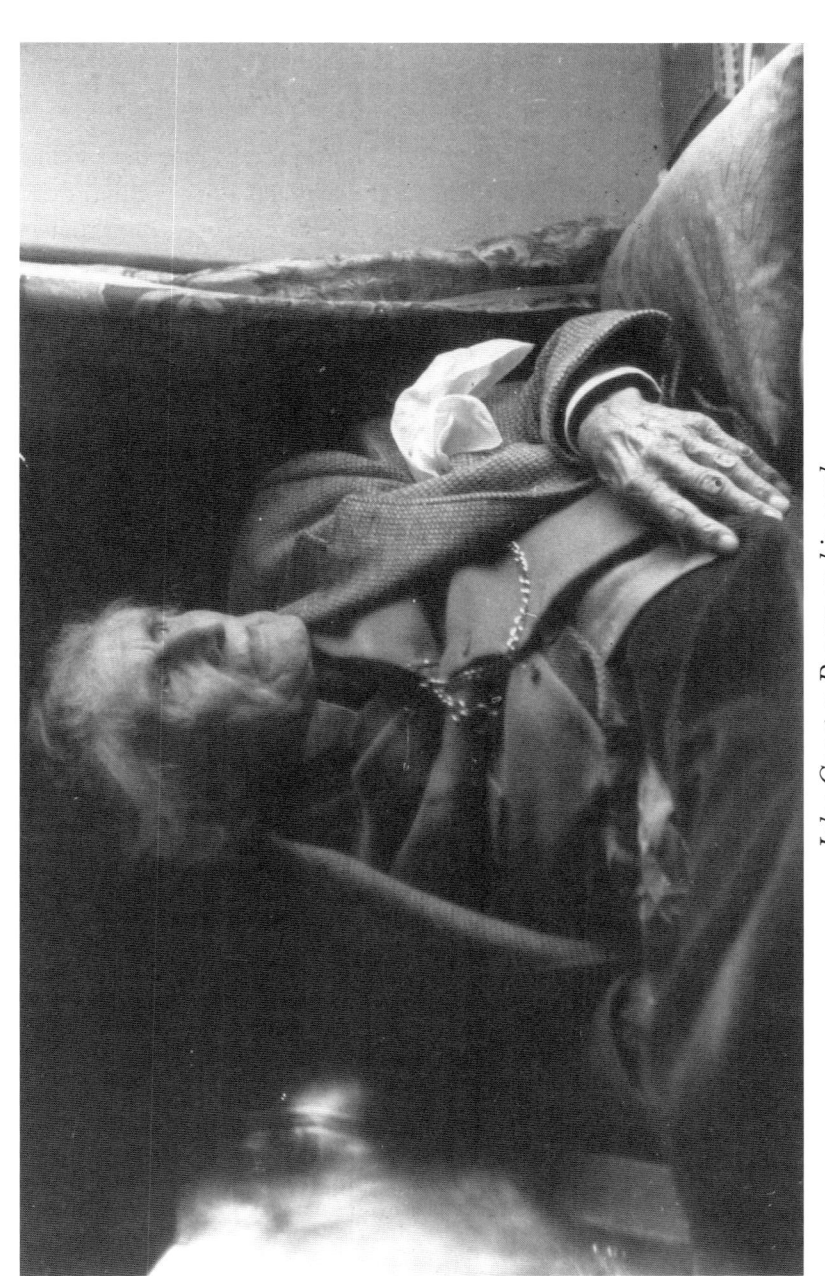

John Cowper Powys on his couch

[*Powys to Purdy 44*]
Sunday July 12th 1959

My dear Jim

I am sending my letter of praise about your <u>Malcolm</u> Book to its Publishers at the same time as I am sending this scrawl to you. I do indeed think feel and <u>know</u> that it's a very remarkable book and I mention the Brontës and Sophocles and Euripides in my praise of it. The boy Malcolm seated on his Bench has something, I tell your publishers, that is really Wordsworthian. O I do my dear friend most heartily congratulate you on this book and I pray that its sale will please its Publishers & reward its author.

We are both well; but we have <u>not</u> had quite enough rain so far to make our Waterfall here as big as I like to see it. But we have had some lovely sunshine. The chief flowers (wild flowers I mean) that I've seen so far are dandelions, buttercups and foxgloves. Oh yes! And lots of roses in the gardens. But to tell you the truth I'm rather thankful to have no garden here.
Yrs affectionately as always
John Cowper Powys Jack
and this brings the best from my Phyllis Playter too.

[*Powys to Lynn Caine*]
July 12th 1959 Sunday

My dear Lynne Caine[48]
I have read James Purdy's 'Malcolm' with the greatest interest and I do indeed think it is a unique work of genius such as nobody but James Purdy could write. The whole idea of the character and tragically brief life of the boy Malcolm is simply wonderful. It has about it that simplified concentration much more like the concentration we get in the Greek Tragedians especially in Sophocles and in Euripides than anything in the more complicated stories of Dickens or Balzac.

The part played in the tale by that <u>Bench</u> on which the boy Malcolm was wont to sit carries with it that special and peculiar influence of the Inanimate upon a human soul which impresses us so in the poetry of Wordsworth. The various characters under whose influence Malcolm comes are so well portrayed that no one could read this book without exclaiming again and again: O how like Mr. So-and-So is Dr Cox the Astrologer with his 'Address'! And again: 'How like Mr and Mrs So-and So are Madame Girard and her husband Mr Girard Girard!' The author has clearly succeeded in doing the one thing that all of us writers are continually – but with what various results! – aiming at doing, namely conveying into the character of the hero some of our own most intimate and secretive reactions to our own life and to the people around us and about us. That longing for his vanished Father and that wild and desperate scene towards the end when for a moment he thinks he has found him have an emotional and super-emotional intensity that makes us think of the Brontë family. One after another as the various characters in the story approach and withdraw, approach again towards, and withdraw again from the ever-waiting Malcolm, yes! the central, ever stationary Malcolm, we get a clearer idea of their personalities and our interest is increased and enhanced in each individual case as we wonder with more and more anxiety what their effect upon the boy will be and what his effect upon them will be. The agitated life of actresses and singers together with the part played by money in their relations with their patrons and audiences is told with a sympathy and understanding that is rare among authors. And there is in this unusual and extraordinary book another topic which plays its heart-rending role in all human intercourse that has been by this author of Malcolm O so wisely adjusted to the extravagantly different temperaments involved in this tale. I need hardly say I refer to sex. The effect upon an immature and extremely simple nature of the sex-appeal, whether exercised in a normal or abnormal way, with a sadistic or masochistic tendency, whether mingled with true love or inspired by momentary attraction, is most penetratingly, tenderly and subtly handled in this weird and unusual book. The little Kermit remains my own favourite character in the story; but the reader of Malcolm need have no favourite. The tale floats and rocks like a boat on that mysterious river of which none of us really know either the beginning or the end, the river of human life upon this earth.[49]

Yrs most sincerely,

John Cowper Powys.

The name Cowper like that of the Poet Cowper is <u>pronounced</u> as if it were Cooper. The Poet himself insisted on this <u>always</u>.

[*Powys to Purdy 45*]
Saturday July 18th 1959

My dear Jim

O I am so glad to hear from you that you, 'your wone self' and that particularly sensitive & subtle lady Mrs Lynne Caine were both so glad to read my letter full of wonder and delight over your 'Malcolm'. Yes I am indeed thankful to learn that Dame Edith felt the same as I do about it and that Carl Van Vechten says he is 'out of his old head' about it! What you say here about the part played by the charwomen and scrubwomen in keeping up the Lights of the New York City Sky-Scrapers interests me extremely – and your words are certainly proved by the fact that there are no lights on Saturday when those excellent folks are not at work. I do indeed pray that your Publisher will find that 'Malcolm' sells well and that that nice sensitive lady Mrs Lynne Caine will be happy about its sale. It is really you know, my dear Jim, a very remarkable work. I am so glad you moved <u>into Brooklyn</u>! I can feel from the way you write that it is just the sort of place to be in that suits you. Well I'll end here willing and wishing wondrous luck to you my dear Jim and to 'MALCOLM'. We have the daily sight out of my window of a darling little toddler called Malcolm who is about two and a half. We persuaded his Mother to bring him up to this room of mine one day. He fell in love with our little girl Doll called Olwen who sits in her chair in the corner near the door. Well!

All good luck my dear Jim from your affectionate old Jack

[*Powys to Purdy 46*]
Tuesday July 21st 1959

My dear Jim

Indeed and indeed & indeed I'll be proud to have your new book 'THE NEPHEW'

<u>DEDICATED</u>

to

<u>me</u>

It is a lovely and startling surprise to think of such an event occurring as that a famous writer & a mysterious Genius should think of dedicating one of his new and eventful WORKS to an old guy like me. O I am so proud that such a thought should have come into your inspired head my dear old pal! You can bet your life it increases my thrilling interest in the thought of actually receiving 'The Nephew' for the Nephew will indeed be <u>my</u> Nephew

I have just written those precious two words the happiest that any writer can ever write yes! THE END I've written at the end of a story entitled 'REAL WRAITHS' about the adventures of <u>Four Ghosts!!</u>

So this is a specially lucky day for me Tuesday July 21st 1959 when I write the <u>END</u> to my latest story and get news of the <u>Dedication</u> of 'The Nephew'. Well! I do pray that 'The <u>Nephew</u>' and also my '<u>Real Wraiths</u>' will <u>both</u> please our publishers by <u>selling well</u>!

May all my pagan deities bless thee and keep thee and show the light of their countenance upon thee all through this year and all through <u>1960</u>.

Yrs always and ever,
John Cowper Powys

O I am so thankful my precious Jim that you moved to <u>Brooklyn</u>!

[*Powys to Purdy 47*]
Tuesday August 25 1959

My dear Jim
    I was so fascinated by <u>Malcolm</u> and so was my Miss Playter too. And O my dear Jim how we are both looking forward to the <u>Nephew</u> and how proud I am to think of it being dedicated to me. There is no doubt about it my dear friend you are a real genius. Yes it was the <u>Loeb Iliad</u> I used as my translation all the way through. I only invented the goddess AEther though AEther is the Homeric name for some special brightness in our sky above Olympus and above Mount Ida and above 'top most Gargarus' as Tennyson calls it. Phyllis Playter is so delighted to think she is going to have her own copy of <u>Malcolm</u> yes I expect it <u>is</u> a bit cooler here than with you but I can tell you its been <u>pretty hot</u> this summer even here! Today we have had the thickest kind of fog which the Welsh call <u>Caddug</u> while they call our most usual and not quite such thick mist <u>Niwl</u> pronounced <u>Niool</u>.
    Well good luck to you old friend and I'm simply longing to read <u>The Nephew</u>.
    yrs always & ever & so says Phyllis John Cowper Powys alias Jack

[*Powys to Purdy 48*]
Tuesday Sept 22nd 1959

    O my dear Jim we are both of us so delighted to hear that Secker and Warburg, one of our VERY BEST Publishers <u>have bought Malcolm</u>. This indeed is <u>grand news</u>. We are both so grateful to you, my dear, for sending us each a separate [copy] of <u>Malcolm</u>. And this indeed is news that the Private Edition of 63 Dream Palace is selling at Bertram Rota's Book Store in London for Sixteen & a half Dollars American money. I love the thought of Malcolm getting a good review in <u>The New York Sunday Times</u>. Yes, my dear, thanks for asking. We are well and doing fine, and <u>greatly tickled</u> by all we read of <u>Mr. K.</u> [Nikita Krushchev] <u>in America</u>!
    Yrs as ever & always John Cowper Powys Jack

[*Powys to Purdy 49*]
Nov 12th 1959

My dear Jim

O I do so heartily yes! in faith heartily congratulate you on this wonderful though I say entirely deserved praise.

Heavens and Earth! But what <u>a splendid lady</u> this Dorothy Parker must be! She does indeed know <u>what's what</u> in the literary world that most difficult of all worlds to steer our way through![50] I am reading again a book I have adored from boyhood Sir Thomas Browne's <u>RELIGIO MEDICI</u> published 1643 but written in 1635. My Miss Phyllis Playter <u>heartily</u> joins me in congratulation! Bravo! You have won!

May my goddesses Hera and Pallas Athene bless you & keep you happy & well – always your devoted old admirer

We've got a tiny toddler of 2 or 3 who waves to me as I look out of my upper window and whose mummy once brought him up to sit on my knee at this window where I <u>lie</u> on my back on a couch and write my books and we have discovered that his name is <u>Malcolm</u>.

[*Purdy to Powys 17*]
236 Henry Street, Brooklyn 1, New York
November 25 (Thanksgiving Eve), 1959

Dear Jack

I was so delighted to have your letter, and was pleased you liked what Miss Dorothy Parker said. I was thrilled, you can imagine.

I also had a nice note from Mr Angus Wilson, informing me that after Mr Gollancz had refused MALCOLM, Mr. Wilson had interceded for me to Secker and Warburg, and that Mrs Warburg is very much taken with MALCOLM. So that is how I got published again in England, through Angus Wilson, who admires you tremendously.[51] I do love the thought of you lying down to write, and I am sure that is the way to do it. Mark Twain wrote nearly everything in bed. There is an interesting passage in Havelock Ellis's autobiography about how he did all his reading lying down, and he ascribed his good health to this. I am pleased you lie down to write. I lie down a great deal.

Also I am delighted you like RELIGIO MEDICI of Sir Thomas Browne. I also admire this, and perhaps even more his HYDRIOTAPHIA OR THE URN-BURIAL, one of the most beautiful things written. There is not a great deal of news. I am continuing writing, or rather, correcting your book THE NEPHEW, and I have written a new short story DADDY WOLF, which I believe ENCOUNTER magazine in London is going to publish.

Dame Edith has been very ill and cannot use her eyes much. I was very excited by the opening of the new Frank Lloyd Wright museum which looks like a big mud-pie made by a giant child![52] Somewhat unfinished looking on the outside, but the inside was just to my taste, spacious and light and rather like going up in a balloon. I wonder if you and Phyllis would have liked it.

My best to you, dear friend my best to you both, Yours ever & ever, Jim.

[*Powys to Purdy 50*]
Monday November 30th 1959

My dear Jim

I had a letter from Guggenheim & Co wanting some words from me in praise of 'Malcolm' in preparation for THE NEPHEW which as you may believe I have heartily given them. I am so sorry to hear from you about Dame Edith's illness, for I do so greatly admire her. O yes! The Every Man's Library edition of Dent & Dutton of Religio Medici by Sir Thomas Browne of Norwich has all his works in it and I fully agree with you that Hydriotaphia or Urn Burial is the finest of all. I keep reading him all the time, if possible aloud to whom ever may be near me for these grand sentences with their unique rhythm sound so well that, as with our Bible, its hard not to read them aloud! I am so glad you like the inside of the new Lloyd Wright Museum. I think we, both of us, would too. I'm delighted you approve so much my writing my books lying on my back and also give me so many kindred examples of it including yourself.

Well my dear Jim all good luck to you and The Nephew and also to

'Daddy Wolf' which I do hope <u>Encounter</u> <u>will</u> publish.
   I love to hear that you have heard from Mr Angus Wilson.
   Always and ever yours JCP & so says Phyllis.

[*Purdy to Powys 18*]
236 Henry Street, Brooklyn 1, New York
December 7, 1959
(Pearl Harbour!)

My dear Jack, dear friend,
   How very kind and helpful that was of you to say a good word for me to the Guggenheims! I do appreciate that. I suppose it is a kind of beggary on my part, but then one can't be too very proud and be an American writer! Americans are not supposed to be writers, and nobody here expects you to be one, so there! Anyhow, my deepest thanks to you.
   I had very good news last week. As Farrar Straus and Cudahy called me in and said right out they had read THE NEPHEW and thought it very remarkable and that if I would make a few minor changes (such as one character who is electrocuted by falling into some telephone wires could not possibly have been electrocuted according to some telephone man they have consulted) they will publish it in September, 1960, and it will be dedicated to him – Robert Giroux – so that the dedication would read DEDICATED TO JOHN COWPER POWYS and to Robert Giroux.[53] I told him I would have to ask you. He pleaded very hard, which was very queer for an editor. Then he said, You know I have gone through hell and high water to get your books published.[54] So I will leave the decision up to you, Jack. I have been reading a very queer book called MARDI by Herman Melville, who was certainly a very peculiar man even for an American writer ... I never cease to marvel at your STRONG CLEAN FIRM Handwriting, Jack ... My very best wishes to you and to Miss Phyllis Playter. Your friend always, and again, heartfelt thanks for speaking to the Guggenheim Consistory.
   Yours ever Jim
PS. That strange Northern land Denmark has purchased <u>Malcolm</u> for Danish translation.[55]

[*Powys to Purdy 51*]
<u>Thursday Dec 10, 1959</u>

My dear Jim

By all means dedicate <u>THE NEPHEW</u> to your Editor as well as to me. I am so delighted and honoured to have the Nephew dedicated to me and to your editor ROBERT GIROUX as well. Those two names Powys and Giroux go very well together.[56] I expect your Publishers of <u>The Nephew</u> were wise not to let that character of yours be electrocuted by falling into telephone wires for it would be a thousand pities if so exciting & remarkable a book should make a technical blunder in such a dramatic life and death kind of situation.

No Jim my dear friend I have never read '<u>Mardo</u>' [*sic*] by Herman Melville but I can well imagine it to be a very exciting book.

But aye! My dear Jim I am so thrilled to hear that <u>Denmark</u> has purchased <u>Malcolm</u> for a Danish translation. I've lately been recalling the time when <u>King Canute</u> of this country <u>sent back his Danish crews and soldiers to Denmark</u> because <u>he got on so very well</u> with Anglo-Saxon courtiers and soldiers. I learnt all that about Canute when I was a boy at school.

No I see they spell Canute <u>CNUT</u> which must be the proper Danish way – but when as a little boy I was taught about King <u>Canute</u> telling his courtiers that no monarch could control the tides of the sea! I always used to associate his personality with that of <u>King Alfred</u> & that tale <u>about his Cakes</u>.

Well! No more margins: so I stop and my Miss Phyllis Playter joins me in sending you united love.

Always your old <u>Jack</u>

CORRESPONDENCE

1960 Powys to Purdy 52-59
Purdy to Powys 19-26

[*Purdy to Powys 19*]
236 Henry Street, Brooklyn 1, New York
February 18 1960

Dear Jack,

    I was so pleased to learn from James Laughlin that he is going to re-publish your stirring AUTOBIOGRAPHY here in New York.[57] I was very happy. I see nearly all your more famous novels in bookstores and libraries, but your AUTOBIOGRAPHY is much harder to find here, though of course it can be found. But now people can have it again.

    I have been a bit under the weather, and so have not written. I think I miss the sun! It is pretty igloo-like here at times in January ... What is your weather in Blaenau like? I am busy revising THE NEPHEW, and I do hope you will like it. They say it is very quiet and terrible. Well, we are what we are, and no amount of rewriting is going to change that!

    Just think this week I am to meet Mr. and Mrs. Warburg, my new English publishers! I will tell you what I think of them! Malcolm appears in England in April 1960!

    Dame Edith wrote me a long and funny letter from Italy, where she is hiding, I gather in her castle. Imagine her living in that immense Castle. I wonder if she roams around in it or sticks to her writing room.

    I do hope you and Phyllis are well, and that everything is going alright there. I heard a very interesting talk on FINNEGANS WAKE by that man who co-authored A SKELETON KEY TO FINNEGANS WAKE, Mr. Henry Robinson.[58] I will close now, dear Jack, with my best wishes to you, my affection and admiration.

    Your friend always
    Jim

[*Powys to Purdy 52*]
Saturday Feb 20 1960

My dear Jim
    I gathered from what was said it was largely owing to your influence that my Autobiography was to be republished in America. I do indeed thank you for this my faithful and true old friend. I love the idea of '<u>The Nephew</u>' being 'very quiet and very terrible'. I sure am longing to have it & so is my lady. I didn't know what <u>igloo</u> was but Phyllis tells me its an Esquimauxs house. It is <u>most exciting</u> my dear to think of your meeting Mr and Mrs Warburg of '<u>Secker and Warburg</u>'. Phyllis has just shown me a picture of Mr Warburg. He looks very unusual and a very remarkable man.
    Its wonderful my dear Jim to think of Malcolm appearing in this country in APRIL. We have only to get to the end of Feb and thro' March & <u>April will be here</u>.
    O yes indeed my dear Jim it certainly is interesting to think of Dame Edith wandering about an enormous Castle in Italy! I'm glad you had that letter from her. Well good luck to you my dear old friend yrs ever. Jack or John Cowper Powys.

[*Purdy to Powys 20*]
236 Henry Street, Brooklyn 1, N.Y.
March 1, 1960.

Dear Jack,
    St. David's day has come and gone! I heard some very interesting Welsh music on my radio, and they told me all about this special Welsh day. Also today in looking at my Gibbon, I came across this passage

> The cavalry of Armorica, the spearmen of Gwent and the archers of <u>Merioneth</u> were equally formidable ...[59]

<u>I liked that very much: the archers of Merioneth</u>, where you live. I liked another thing Gibbon says very much: 'The malicious Welshman insinuates that the English taciturnity might possibly be the effect of their servitude under the Normans.'

Today I had very good news, for the publication firm of GALLIMARD in Paris, have purchased MALCOLM, for French translation.⁶⁰ They paid a very fine sum, so that I shall be eating regularly at least until summer! I cook nearly all my own meals and eat lots of <u>mush</u>. Do you have mush there? I bet nobody has it but Americans, and they don't anymore.

It is very cold here, which is not to my liking, as I can't very well watch my ships go to South America.

Dame Edith returns to that ladies' club in London, Sesame and Imperial this month. She told me a mad young poet came to see her there and threatened to take off all his clothes in front of her guests, but at the last moment he got cold feet … Well, I must close. I think of you each day and send you my affectionate greetings, Yours ever, Jim & sincere greetings to Phyllis.

[*Powys to Purdy 53*]
Saturday, March 5th 1960

Dear Jim

Yes indeed you sure do quote Gibbon well. O I do adore old Gibbon from the bottom of my heart. That story of how he knelt down to kiss a lady's hand and couldn't get up again till she stooped over him and helped him up. How well I recall that particular Arch at Rome built by one of the Emperors that made him as he looked long and long & long at it decide to write his great Book. Yes there <u>may</u> be something in that remark about our taciturnity (I speak as an Englishman for all my ancestral Welsh blood!) being due to the tyranny of those Norman Barons in their Castles.

O my dear Jim I am so glad to hear of the Publishing Firm of Gallimard in Paris having purchased your <u>Malcolm</u> for French translation and paid you a good round sum for it. Just think of your cooking your own meals! I must ask my Miss Phyllis Playter to tell me just what the exact meaning of the word <u>Mush</u> is!⁶¹

Think of that young Poet threatening to take off his clothes in front of all the Ladies in Dame Edith's club in London – <u>Sesame and Imperial</u>.

Yes I agree too about <u>Ike's</u> Tour.⁶² Yes! There is really something rather QUIXOTIC about it all. <u>I like Ike</u>. All the best from us both my dear – ever & always your loyal old John Cowper Powys.

[*Purdy to Powys 21*]
236 Henry Street, Brooklyn 1, New York, USA
April 21, 1960

My dear Jack,

    I have not written sooner as I have been going through the pains of perdition trying to finish THE NEPHEW, which my editor says is the only book ever written in which nothing happens and in which the material nonethelesss entirely shatters the mind of the reader. They say some people's hair turns entirely white when they read it. I have also written a new short story called GOODNIGHT, SWEETHEART.

    My editor has taken a vacation.

    I am so glad the sun is out and I can walk about and see the ships and dogs and cats and animals at the zoo. Winter will not do for poor people.

    Mr Warburg writes me that he has got my first book of stories away from Mr. Gollancz and he is going to publish it again with all the words that Mr. Gollancz's prudish hands would not let him print. I gather Mr Warburg is not very friendly with Mr. Gollancz. I do not know whether Dame Edith hit Gollancz over the head with her cane or not, but she told me she was giving it a good deal of thought.

    MALCOLM appears in your England, Jack, on April 28 – a week from today.

    What is new in Wales? I bet you have beautiful weather there now, and I suppose the sheep are in pastures.

    I should tell you that the Ford Foundation, one of the richest in the world, has granted me a fellowship to pursue my writing, and so I am grateful to them and to you for recommending me. The Guggenheims, therefore, asked me to relinquish their fellowship as they felt, I gather, that with two, I would be apt to become a plutocrat and take to doing nothing at all!

    I am toiling away through the entire <u>Decline and Fall of the Roman Empire</u>. The footnotes, though death to read, are among the most rewarding. I like the one where Gibbon says he has had a happy life, for he has found his joy in his work.

Do write me your news, dear Jack, my best to you, dear friend, and my sincerest wishes to Miss Phyllis Playter. Yours ever Jim

[*Powys to Purdy 54*]
Thursday April 28th 1960

My dear Jim

Just think of this being the very actual date when I am reading your letter to me written by you on April 21st. I am so very very interested about the 'Nephew' 'in which nothing happens but the material shatters the minds of the reader.'

Just think of Mr Warburg having got your 1st book of stories away from Mr Gollancz. I wonder if Dame Edith did have anything to do with it! I love to think of your seeing ships, dogs, cats and zoo animals as you walk out. The Ford Foundation has granted you a Fellowship to pursue your writing.

Alas, my dear all the news I've got for you about Miss Playter and me is rather annoying, for both of us have got Asian Flu which has left me so weak I can hardly walk a step and has left Phyllis with an annoying cough – yrs ever John Cowper & Phyllis sends her love.

[*Purdy to Powys 22*]
236 Henry Street, Brooklyn, N.Y., USA

June 7, 1960

My dear Jack,

I was so sorry to hear that you had been sick with that terrible Asiatic Flu, which I have had off and on, too, and I know how dreadful it is. One is completely powerless when it gets you down. Nothing to do but groan! I do hope you and Miss Playter are much better.

I do think I have finished THE NEPHEW, and my editor thinks so, too, though he is sniffing here and sniffing there, and looking about to see if I have made any mistakes or said anything too utterly impossible for the public. Just think, this is YOUR book I do hope you will like it. It is all about aunts and uncles and nephews and small town gossip.

Did you by any chance see the nice review of MALCOLM in the (London) Times Literary Supplement for May 6, and the (London) Times for April 28. Dame Edith sent them to me.

I do so look forward to your new book ALL OR NOTHING and hope it will find many readers and admirers.

I am already on a new opus, which seems to be all DIALOGUE.

By chance I [fell] upon some little pieces of sermons by Jeremy Taylor, which were very exciting, and I must get his complete works and read them. I read these snippets in old Hippolyte Taine's History of English Literature, a book I like. It is said to be hopelessly out of date, which is probably why I enjoy it.

Soon New Directions will be re-publishing your grand AUTO-BIOGRAPHY.

Do write me your news, and I hope this finds you both much better, and enjoying a Welsh summer!

I have not written sooner owing to the plague of correcting all my mistakes in the typescript of THE NEPHEW.

With affectionate wishes, and a prayer for your good health. Your friend always & always, Jim

[*Powys to Purdy 55*]
Monday June 13th 1960

My dear Jim

Yes! I saw those notices in the Times and also I saw a <u>Picture of you there</u>. And I think but I <u>may</u> be putting my wishes and hopes in place of an actual vision I <u>think</u> I saw that Marie Canavaggia the famous French translator who translated my <u>Jobber Skald</u> – or did I call that 'Wood and Stone'? – a book all about Weymouth Beach and Portland and Chesil Beach and Maiden Castle and Thomas Hardy – was going to translate your Malcolm into French. She and her sister Renee come from Causicaa, as Napoleon did! Renee is a famous Astronomer. Have I spelt Causica wrong? Ought it to be <u>Corsica</u>? Yes! I think it ought to be. So I <u>did</u> spell it wrong. Yes my book 'All or Nothing' published by

Macdonald 16 Maddox St London W.1. is <u>out</u> but so far they've only sent me <u>one</u> copy instead of the usual six they send their authors. So I can't at the moment give any copies away to my friends and relatives.

    I am yours always and ever <u>Jack</u> otherwise <u>John Cowper Powys</u>
Yes thanks we are better. But I am still awfully weak and can't walk outside the house. I am now just finishing a book entitled '<u>Abertackle</u>' but so far it has not been typed at all. Abertackle is the name of the village from which the hero of my Book, whose name is Gor, comes. But I have still got several typed new Stories <u>ready</u> for <u>Publication</u>. They are <u>Topsy Turvy</u>, <u>You and Me</u>, <u>The Three Wraiths</u> and another one whose name at the moment I have forgotten.

[*Purdy to Powys 23*]
236 Henry Street, Brooklyn 1, New York, USA
August 13, 1960

My dear Jack,

    I have very good news. Mr Frederic Warburg, the Head of Martin Secker and Warburg Publishers, has read and liked tremendously my book THE NEPHEW and will of course publish it. His wife Pamela de Bayou also liked it tremendously. This is the book I have dedicated to you and so naturally I was eager that my English publisher should think well of it. Mr Warburg thinks it is my best book. A copy of it will be coming to you shortly. I have ordered your new novel ALL OR NOTHING and hope it gets here soon.

    Last night I saw the new American balloon satellite flying over the New York skyline. I was completely surprised as I had no idea I would be able to see it. It looked rather tired, I thought, and going at great effort. It also looked quite man-made and nothing like a moon or star.

    I am at work on my play. I hope you are feeling better and are writing on a new book. Angus Wilson is coming to America in October and he will be sure to see me, and I will give you a report of our meeting. Write me soon, and let me know the news. Your friend, always and always, with affectionate wishes to you and Miss Playter.

    Yours Jim

[*Powys to Purdy 56*]
Tuesday August 16th 1960

My dear Jim

This is indeed grand news and my Miss Phyllis Player and I are both delighted to hear that <u>The Nephew</u> the Book dedicated to me is going to be published now. We are longing to read it. Think of your seeing the New American Balloon Satellite flying over the New York Skyline. You beat us there my dear. Neither of us have caught a glimpse of it. I am so glad to hear that Angus Wilson is coming to America in October & I am looking forward to hearing from you an account of your meeting. I am so proud you've ordered my '<u>All or Nothing</u>' and I pray you'll get it soon. I ought to have sent it to you.

Well, my dear Jim, <u>our</u> best news is that a week ago we had a visit from my Publishers the Boss of Macdonalds who is the owner of it now for there are no Macdonalds left in the Firm. My friend and patron is Mr. Eric Harvey whose wife's name is Phyllis. They brought with them to see us their youngest children a pair of twins called Juliet and Richard. Richard and I got on so well we'll be friends for life. We have also had a recent visit from Redwood Anderson and his wife Gwyneth who now live in Essex but they have a cottage near here whither they will be often visiting us for a couple of months I know, before they return to Essex.[64]

Yes I've written about three more <u>Space-Travel books</u> which have been typed and I hope will appeal to Mr Eric Harvey when he reads them.

Miss Playter can go 'down-town' as we call it, shopping now since our attack of <u>Asian Flu</u> but I am still too weak to leave the house although early every afternoon I come up the eleven steps of our little staircase and lie on my back at the window watching the lights of the Hydro-Electric scheme go up and down.

This, my dear Jim, brings you all my affection. We have a French girl friend called Mlle Marie Canavaggia who is I hope going to translate the Nephew into French.

CORRESPONDENCE

[*Powys to Purdy 57*]
September 1st 1960 Thursday

My dear Jim

I am so thrilled and so is my Phyllis to have your 'Nephew' safe & sure in my Book case here in my reading and writing room. I have just got as far as Division 4 The Professor which I have begun to read with the greatest excitement. O I did so love to see this splendid Book dedicated to my own very self together with Robert Giroux.

Both Miss Playter and I are fast recovering from our recent attack of Asian Flu tho' we are still equally ignorant as to just whither this Flu in Asia started. But until 4 days ago I suffered from this Flu a feeling of such hopeless weakness that I thought I should never leave this little house again but I am really better now. Miss Phyllis Playter helped me to make the effort and all the four recent mornings Saturday Monday Tuesday I have been for a little stroll, sitting down at intervals on various stones on the way till I reached in my walk today the great wheel at the foot of our big waterfall.

yrs always & ever John Cowper Powys.

[*Purdy to Powys 24*]
236 Henry Street, Brooklyn 1, New York
October 27, 1960

My dear Jack,

I have not written as I have been sick in bed with – I do believe – the same affliction you suffered from, Asiatic Flu – perhaps it is a dilute form of the Great Plague. I have conjunctivitis in one eye from it, so that I look as if I had been in a fight. I do hope you are better and getting back your strength.

THE NEPHEW has finally been published here, and has received a great deal of praise. Dame Edith Sitwell has called it 'a great book … a masterpiece'. And Angus Wilson also praised it. I have not read all the reviews, as it is still being reviewed, for it was only published 2 weeks ago, when I was ill.

Do gain back your strength, I think of you so often dear friend, Yours, with affectionate wishes, Ever, Jim

[*Powys to Purdy 58*]
[undated: early November 1960?]

My dear Jim

  We are both so shocked that you have had <u>Asian Flu</u> and now have got conjunctivitis. We had a fine visit the other day from the present Boss of Macdonalds my Publishers. His name is Eric Harvey and he lives in Bath Somerset. There are no more Macdonalds left in the Firm but he uses their name now that he has bought them out. By an interesting chance his wife's name is Phyllis. Phyllis came with him which delighted my Miss Phyllis Playter and they brought their two youngest children who are Twins aged Seven Richard and Juliet and I got on O so well with Richard, <u>so well</u> that I have written to him since their visit. We had a letter from Marie Canavaggia this morning who is so delighted to have had your copy of your 'Nephew'. She is hard at work in translating Malcolm and thinks she has struck the right note now after some preliminary work that did not satisfy her. She tells us she has sent you the address for the gallery in New York where her sister (Jeanne)'s Paintings can be visited. We wish that you could go and see them but we doubt that you will be well enough. They <u>are</u> interesting Yes! O such an interesting family of three sisters – Marie is the literary one Renee is an astronomer in the Observatoire in Paris and Jeanne is the Painter. Their parents are dead. Like Napoleon all came from Corsica. We are looking forward to the publication of 'the Nephew' over here and wishing it with all our prayers a grand reception.

[*Purdy to Powys 25*]
236 Henry Street, Brooklyn 1, New York
November 26, 1960

My dear Jack,

  Here I am in the land of the living again, and am writing a new book about a man who got out of the penitentiary and fell in love with two women at the age of 42.

  Just as I was sitting here about to go for a walk who should call on the telephone but Angus Wilson! He is here in New York City to give some lectures. We both spoke of you, and he is, of course one of your profoundest admirers.

I had a wonderful letter in French from Mlle. Marie Canavaggia, and I am so grateful to you that you put me in touch with her. I enjoyed her letter very much, and I replied to her half in French and half in English! I also wrote a young American man who lives in Paris to go to Mlle Canavaggia, with his wife, and explain to her what certain words in 'Malcolm' meant, for they were American words she said she could not find in the dictionary. The young man and his wife went and met Mlle Canavaggia and her sister, and they had a good time talking.

I was very sad though if she put off translating your 'Autobiography' for 'Malcolm' but perhaps I misunderstood her French.

We are not having any Fall weather at all this year. Or rather all the weather is out of the September calendar, and the sun shines, the birds sing, and we do not need heat in the buildings. I have been taking lots of walks and also going to the night court to hear the petty criminals on trial, as the language there is that good rich American talk, as it seems only the old American stock is arrested. The Jews and Italians and Poles are not so often arrested, but the Negroes and the Americans from the South are often on trial for things like vagrancy, street-walking, stealing apples, striking men in saloons, or exposing oneself in public and of course what they say and the police who arrested them say and the judge's warnings are all – to me – interesting but maybe nobody else would find it so.

I think of you, dear Jack, every day. Before I forget I am reading Ovid's Metamorphoses in Latin, a few lines a day. I hope you are at work on your new novel, Mr Bumpus has never sent me your 'All or Nothing', which I ordered months ago, so I have ordered it from another publisher or rather bookstore here in New York.[65] I will tell you what Angus Wilson says and does.

Your friend, always. Jim

Dame Edith wrote how when they asked her if they could come and film 'Lady Chatterley's Lover' at Renishaw for a movie she dared them to come for she would be on the roof ready to throw rocks at them.

[*Powys to Purdy 59*]
Sunday Dec 4th 1960

My dear Jim

I am thrilled to hear of this new Book you are writing about a man aged 42 who got out of the Penitentiary and fell in love with two women – and all this in what you so well describe as 'the Land of the living'. Just think of Angus Wilson having come to lecture in New York City and being near you. Please give him my love and best wishes. Aye! But that is amusing what you tell me Dame Edith said when they wanted to film 'Lady Chatterley's Lover' at Renishaw.

I love to think of you being in touch with Mlle Marie Canavaggia and her sister Renee in Paris and that your American couple went to see her & explained those American expressions in Malcolm that weren't in the Dictionary. I am so interested too in what you say about the petty criminals in that Night Court – where the Jews, and Italians and Poles aren't arrested as often as the Americans and Negroes of the South.

I do hope and pray you get my 'All or Nothing' from that Book Shop. Aye! My dear Jim! But I do so love to think of your reading Ovid in Latin. Good luck to you!

We are going to send you a Paper Back Book published by Penguin and Pelican Books entitled Poets in Landscape by Gilbert Highet which includes Catullus Virgil Horace Propertius Tibullus Ovid and Juvenal – a book which I have learnt O such a lot from and have enjoyed so much.

Yrs always John Cowper Powys

[*Purdy to Powys 26*]
236 Henry Street, Brooklyn 1, New York
December 10, 1960

My dear Jack,

I am sending you a story called 'Daddy Wolf', which is based on the 'confession' of one of the petty criminals I heard at the Night Court. You may find it to your taste.

Christmas is coming with all its monstrous confusion, and if I were a bird I would fly off to one of the West Indies, one of the ones not blowing up in a revolution. I do admire, though, Fidel Castro, for taking away all that property the Americans owned, and giving it back to the Cubans, where it really belonged. I am going to write you a real letter, soon, but I thought I would send you 'Daddy Wolf' which horrified the publishers, the old farts, nearly all of them. I am tired of grown up people being horrified, but if they weren't maybe there would be no point in us being writers.

    I am awaiting 'All or Nothing', but the mails have gone mad owing to Christmas.

    My best affection to you and my best wishes to Miss Playter. Yours ever, Jim.

1961   Powys to Purdy 60-67
           Purdy to Powys 27-32

[*Powys to Purdy 60*]
[These appear to be two versions of one letter, presumably both by accident mailed together.]
Friday Jan 6th 1961

My dear Jim

    The Xmas rush is the cause of my not answering your Dec 10th 1960 letter <u>earlier than this</u> with its wonderful story of <u>Daddy Wolf</u>. Both of us Phyllis and I your old Jack are thrilled by it. Phyllis has sent you a copy of '<u>All or Nothing</u>' which we hope will reach you before the one you ordered.

Five minutes to Four

My dear Jim

    Here I am <u>upstairs</u> in my writing–room in Trousers and big Slippers. Here is your wonderful Story entitled <u>Daddy Wolf</u> sent to us on Dec 10th 1960. It has been the Xmas rush that has prevented me from answering before this your letter of Dec 10th 1960 with this wonderful story called <u>Daddy Wolf</u>. You sure are a real genius for Story-telling. Few, <u>if any</u>, can equal you.

[*Purdy to Powys 27*]
236 Henry Street, Brooklyn
Friday, February 6 1961

My dear Jack,
 Here I am snowed in under 18 inches of snow, eating canned salmon and Finnish bread, and not going out. New York is paralyzed – the worst weather since 1881 since Walt Whitman!
 I adored your 'All or Nothing' – and especially enjoyed it on the blizzardy nights; a demi-god-Grandfather was telling me this tale and I like it one of the best of all your things. Thank you so much for 'All or Nothing' with its beautiful sentences and wonderful personages and thank you for the Gilbert Highet book – very informative. Of course he does not have your insight into classical literature and I gather he is a Calvinist and likes money.[66] The only Calvinist I ever would endure was Herman Melville who was punished by having to love his own sex in secret. I broke my typewriter and so am without that – hence my pen.
 I was thrilled you and Miss Playter like my story 'Daddy Wolf'. But 'All or Nothing' has been my blizzard-companion.
 Today the sun is out and beginning to melt the high trenches of snow. Poor old <u>ENGLOUTIE</u> Brooklyn – so citified the snow abandons it like a jungle, all New York has gone down under the elements – hurrah! Ghosts are now far from invisible – also cats prowl.
 My publisher bought me the magnificent complete and unabridged Latin Oxford dictionary founded on Andrews' Edition of Freund and revised and enlarged by Messrs Lewis and Short. It has all Latin words holy, obscene and kitchen commonplace. Thank you [for] your masterful 'All or Nothing', Love Jim.

[*Powys to Purdy 61*]
Tuesday Feb 28th 1961

'EXPECTATION'

My dear Jim
 This is the day which in my 'Collins' One Day Royal Diary' I always

call by <u>the name of the Stick</u> which I always carried for my walk, namely EXPECTATION.

Tomorrow will be called by the name of another of my Sticks namely '<u>HOO-DOO</u>' a stick of dark ebony which also came from America. I have such affectionate fondness for my sticks that I regulate my life by their names. My own favourite of all Dictionaries is my Oxford Greek one and I am very fond too of my Oxford Latin one. My own university was <u>not</u> Oxford but Cambridge. Cambridge is much more individualistic than Oxford. Oxford is made up of <u>groups</u> of graduates and undergraduates whereas Cambridge has only its individual great men. Our greatest Cambridge poet was Milton and our greatest scientist was Sir Isaac Newton and our greatest Humorist was Lawrence Sterne with his <u>Tristram Shandy</u>. The writer I am most grateful to Oxford for is <u>Matthew Arnold</u> for I adore his poetry but I wish to the Devil that his Daddy Head-Master of Rugby had sent him to Cambridge rather than to Oxford but I <u>ought not to wish that</u> – for Matthew Arnold's best friend was Arthur Hugh Clough, whom he met at Oxford.

Well, Jim old friend, I must stop now for it's about four o' clock.

O yes! And my favourite poet after Shakespeare and Milton has always been Wordsworth and before they both died & were buried together in the Roman Catholic Cemetery in Bath Somersetshire, my only wife and my only son gave me a volume of Wordsworth on whom I lectured at Cockermouth where he was born long before I ever crossed to America or ever saw Philadelphia my favourite of all cities.

[*Powys to Purdy 62*]
MARCH 20th 1961

My dear Jim

Your Book 'Colour of Darkness' came on Saturday, sent by <u>Publishers Secker and Warburg</u> and Phyllis & I were so pleased to read all the good reviews of it and of all your works in yesterday's SUNDAY PAPERS. This morning the April number of <u>Encounter</u> came and the whole back Cover of the Magazine had only your three books on it, namely <u>Malcolm</u>, <u>the Nephew</u> and <u>Colour of Darkness</u>. You will no doubt in any case see all these but I am enclosing them and perhaps they will reach you before any others. Phyllis and & I are now both of us in my room up the eleventh step of our little staircase. She is burning papers in the fire-pit and up the chimney: We have had a letter from Marie Canavaggia saying that [she] has just taken her finished translation of Malcolm to Gallimard the Publisher. She is now going to translate, also for Gallimard, my Autobiography.[67] So you see that though we've never met and are so far apart ourselves in Brooklyn New York and North Wales our writings are now close together in Paris. We hear that Gamel and Gerald Brenan are leaving for Rome on next Sunday (Palm Sunday) on their way to Greece. I think Edith Sitwell's introduction to your Book was splendid.

yrs ever & always John Cowper Powys.

[*Purdy to Powys 28*]
236 Henry Street, Brooklyn 1, New York
March 25, 1961

My dear Jack,

How thrilled I was to get your fine letter and to hear about your different walking sticks, and to visualize you and Miss Phyllis Playter reading the reviews of my book up your eleven steps to your reading room, and that she was burning old papers. I do so like a fireplace where one can burn papers and woods, and though I have a fireplace it is defunct.

I was simply open-mouthed with astonishment when I read Mr John Davenport's review of COLOUR OF DARKNESS and THE NEPHEW in that large powerful OBSERVER! Dame Edith was so overjoyed that she cablegraphed me from London. Just imagine.

Just think, dear Jack, you and dear Dame Edith were the first to see anything in me at all! That is why I dedicated THE NEPHEW to you and COLOUR OF DARKNESS to her! I loved her preface to my book and am glad you like it too. She is very ill in London and I am worried about her!

I have been rather cross and grumpy because our weather is so terrible, no sun and rain, sleet, all the demons seem in charge of the weather. It's all explained in Ovid's Metamorphoses, which I am plodding along in in the original Latin.

I have also written a short play but it has no title, and a producer said he wanted to put it on the stage. It only lasts an hour, but he said that it was all any audience could stand, they would all go home and get drunk after it was over.

I had a fine letter from Gerald Brenan last week, just before he went to Greece, with his wife Gamel.

I am so glad that Marie Canavaggia finished her translation of MALCOLM. She can now do a more important book, your marvelous AUTOBIOGRAPHY, which I just a day ago saw in a fine bookstore in Greenwich village.

Thank you again for sending me the wonderful John Davenport review. Hurrah!

My best wishes to Miss Playter, and all good thoughts and affection, dear Jack.

Yours ever and ever, Jim

[*Purdy to Powys 29*]
236 Henry Street, Brooklyn 1, New York USA
June 1, 1961

Dear Jack,

Here it is June already, and we had no spring, we plunged from winter to summer. I have begun a new novel called CABOT WRIGHT BEGINS, which concerns a well-known rapist, who ravished nearly 300 women before he was caught. My publisher is somewhat sad I have chosen this, but gradually he has grown used to the idea, and now he is enthusiastic about what he has read. I never can believe I will finish any of the books I begin, they are so hard for me to do, and then step by step, day by day, somehow they are all written, perhaps done by a force hidden in the keys or the wood of the writing table.

I have wondered how you are, and what you are doing. I think of your wooden walking sticks, very often, sometimes when I am lying down to go to sleep. Do write me if you feel so inclined. Soon it will be very hot and I will have to close the shutters tight to keep out the heat.

My best to you, dear Jack, I think of you so very often, Yours ever and ever, with affection. Jim

[*Powys to Purdy 63*]
June 6th 1961

My dear Jim

Your NEW NOVEL entitled 'CABOT WRIGHT BEGINS' based on a well-known young rapist who ravished nearly three hundred women before he was caught does indeed sound to me extremely exciting. I've been lately very hard at work writing a new Preface to my long novel called <u>WOLF SOLENT</u> which I wrote when my father and <u>his</u> Father lived at STALBRIDGE a village with a Railway Station between Sherborne and Yeovil, Sherborne containing both the Preparatory School and the Big School of one of the best Public Schools in this country.

Yours ever and always. John Cowper Powys

[*Purdy to Powys 30*]
236 Henry Street, Brooklyn, New York
July 8, 1961

My dear Jack

I had sent off to you today a gift which I hope you will like and which I hope you will consider 'Magic'. I do hope it will prove so.

I am enjoying summer and trees and being out of doors all the time as much as I can with the 'contract' for my new novel hanging over my head; I never feel I will live through another book, they are too horrible! Still, I manage to.

A professor of English literature from Chicago, who stops by here from time to time is a great admirer of yours, and especially WOLF SOLENT, which he said was one of the greatest emotional experiences of his life when he read it, and he will be very pleased and excited when he knows you are writing a new introduction to it. His name is Napier Wilt.[68]

I had a very nice letter from Gerald Brenan, who has sent me a very fascinating novel he has written called A HOLIDAY BY THE SEA; he has been to Greece, but then I imagine you have heard all about it, from him or his wife.

I will close now as I have this deep-seated depression over writing a new novel, and all the sunshine in the world isn't going to help. In winter one expects to be depressed!

Do write me if you feel the inclination. What ever became of the toddler named Malcolm who lives near you? Yours ever and ever, your friend, Jim

PS Do let me know if you get my gift and if you think it may be 'magic'. It is from a store called Brooks Brothers.

[*Powys to Purdy 64*]
July 14th 1961

My dear Jim

I am indeed most interested to hear of the Professor from Chicago whose name is Napier Wilt. Please give him my blessing the next time you see him.

Your gift has not yet arrived but we are eagerly awaiting its arrival. We have had a visit from professor Ichiro Hara of Tokyo JAPAN who is a great admirer of Wordsworth & is making a special tour to study the Wordsworthian Lake District and the Poet's movements there.

We have got that book of Gerald Brenan '<u>Holiday by the Sea</u>'. But we have not read it yet.

Yours ever and always John Cowper Powys.

[*Powys to Purdy 65*]
August 2nd 1961 Wednesday

My dear Jim

Thank you a thousand times for this wonderful magic stick. It strikes me as having such great power in it that it may eventually persuade me to break the decision I had made in my own mind not to leave the little Half-House of ours and climb up the narrow path to the foot of the

Woollen-Mill Wheel and the big Waterfall till the end of the month. Now I hold in my hands the present time volume of '<u>ENCOUNTER</u>' edited by Stephen Spender and Melvin J. Laski. And I have to face <u>W.H. Auden</u> and the <u>Alienated City</u>.

Well! My dear Jim, this is yours with great gratitude.

<u>Jack</u> or John Cowper Powys.

[*Purdy to Powys 31*]
236 Henry Street, Brooklyn 1, New York, USA
October 8 1961

My dear friend,

I have been getting up at 5:00 AM now in order to see Venus, now observable at that hour, and also my favorite constellation Orion; his belt of three stars at the present time is very clear. Saturn and Jupiter are also beautiful earlier in the evening. I spend nearly all evenings on the roof of this old house looking out to sea and to the sky.

It was such a pleasure to hear you had received and liked the Magic Cane made of moonstuff. I hope you do take walks; a walk about the room with it is quite producing in all kinds of spells.

My book is going ahead, and since I have such a small audience, I am not taking any pains to spare that audience's sensibilities, this time at all, if ever I did before. I am writing it exactly as I please and to the lowest hell with America … I am very pleased I have this roof to go to, as I was getting very tired of my room, which I share with a Finnish chemist, who is almost certainly an alchemist to boot; you know all Finns practice witchcraft, and are noted witches. Did you by chance see the eclipse of the Moon? It turned brown like a sea-urchin. And looked also spiny. I do hope you and Miss Playter are well, and that you will be writing to me before too long; I long for your letters; winter is coming and the only good thing about it is it will bring Orion and his belt to the early evening sky, and I can gaze to my heart's content. I have a small telescope, by the way.

Your devoted friend, with love to you both
  James Purdy.
Dame Edith is living in a flat in Green Hill, Hampstead.

[*Powys to Purdy 66*]
Nov 5th 1961

    We are both ever so grateful for your letter and your news that Dame Edith is living in a flat in Green Hill Hampstead London. Yes indeed I am grateful for this magic cane made of moonstuff. I haven't yet dared to carry it as far as the foot of our big Waterfall up on the hill behind our house where the huge red wheel of the Welsh Woollen Mill turns and where I used to sit on a low stone wall. But I hope I'll be brave enough to do so ere so very long for I do long to see that woollen mill wheel again.

    We love to think of you spending your time on your roof looking at Venus and at Orion with his belt. We are so glad to hear you have a small telescope. I am however very glad at what you tell me about the fact that this wonderful <u>Magic Cane</u> made of moonstuff you gave me can produce a lot of its spells by merely being carried up and down our room without going out of doors at all. NO we didn't see the Eclipse of the Moon. But O we do <u>so love</u> to think of you looking at Orion and his belt in the early evening sky. We are thrilled to think of you gazing at Orion and his belt. Please remember that we <u>never</u> forget all that you and nobody else but you have done for our experience of life by yes! By all you have <u>told</u> us and <u>explained</u> to us. The part you have played in our life my friend has been great. I do trust <u>your book</u> will bring you honour & glory –

    yrs ever John Cowper Powys.

[*Purdy to Powys 32*]
236 Henry Street, Brooklyn 1, New York USA
November 11 [1961] (Armistice Day!)

My dear friend,

    I was so terribly thrilled to get your beautiful letter, it is very touching, and I am deeply grateful if I have added anything to your enjoyment by my letters; I cannot tell you how wonderful, more than wonderful it has been to know you and hear from you from far off Wales, and to have your letters as well as your great books at hand.

I was so very interested in hearing about the Welsh Woollen Mill, and I do hope you may go there before the weather gets too cold out.

Some time ago I sent you a new anthology compiled by NEW DIRECTIONS, which contains some poems and stories by me, specially one called SERMON, which you may possibly be interested in. Dame Edith told me, that after her first surprise at SERMON, she liked it very much.

I hear Osbert Sitwell had a brain operation here in the USA for multiple sclerosis, which has afflicted him for some time, but I have not heard from Dame Edith about it.

Each evening I continue to admire Orion, Jupiter and Saturn (the latter two now retreating as winter deepens), and in the early morning just before the sun rises, Venus and Mercury together, a breathtaking sight.

Yes, dear friend, I think of you often, and send you my magicest thoughts, and my abiding appreciation.

Yours ever and ever, Jim

PS My one-act play 'Children is All' about a mother and her son from the penitentiary, has been accepted for publication by Street and Smith's 'Mademoiselle', which published Dylan Thomas!

[*Powys to Purdy 67*]
Dec 4 1961 [postmark]

My dear friend of friends

I was very glad to have your letter and I received the copy of New Directions and I enjoyed your stories in it very much: and your poem too.

Winter has begun here. We have had it yesterday and today. The snow has come three quarters of the way down the mountain but we didn't have any on the ground. People struggled to do their Christmas shopping amid gales of rain & sleet: But today being Sunday the streets are empty and everyone is at home by their fire. I have not yet had the Courage to climb the Hill carrying that beautiful silvery Moon-white stick you gave me but I can see that precious stick waiting in the corner of our room till the time of my courage arrives. I am so glad your one-act play 'children is all' has been accepted by Street and Smith for their Magazine Mademoiselle.

1962 Powys to Purdy 68
Purdy to Powys 33-34

[*Purdy to Powys 33*]
236 Henry Street, Brooklyn 1, New York
February 2, 1962

My dear friend,

   I am eagerly waiting until the constellation of BOOTES will rise early enough for me to see him, along side URSA MAJOR, for now one can't see BOOTES until well past midnight, and I am too sleepy to go up to the roof and watch him. When Orion sets earlier and earlier it is a sure sign Winter is waning. We have not had too bad a winter this year but I believe you may be having an extreme one. I was sure we would all have been blown up by now by the Russians, but here we still are looking up at the constellations in their nightly progress.

   I am slowly finishing my new novel CABOT WRIGHT BEGINS and have also written a short dramatic piece called CRACKS which concerns an 80-year old woman in Virginia who imagines she talks with God just, as a matter of fact, when Jupiter is in the summer sky.

   I heard that Dame Edith was hard-up for money and was selling her paintings, I have not heard from her since last year.

   I do hope this short letter finds you and Miss Playter well.

   I read a book which somewhat interested me last week, not a new book, EVELYN INNES by George Moore. Now I am reading an older one than that, LEVIATHAN by Hobbes, which has a style I rather like.

   Please write and tell me what you are doing. I long for spring. These cold nights make me ache, and I can't get out to see the ships frequently enough.

   Your friend who sends you affection, Always, Jim

This building I live in is frequently broken into by Burglars, but they have spared my room so far, probably because they know I practice WITCHCRAFT!

[*Powys to Purdy 68*]
February 19 1962

My dear friend

It seems quaint that though we are both writing to each other in February I should be writing on February 19th and you on February 2nd and both of us in the year 1962. We had a very hard winter at the beginning of it and Phyllis was made ill by it but I have kept well all the time. I never cared much for George Moore but I agree with you that Hobbes' 'LEVIATHAN' is a fine book. I read it again a few years ago and I like it more than ever. It is good news to hear you are <u>finishing</u> your new novel; for that means it may not be so long before we can read it. I think that play of yours about the Old Lady talking to God when Jupiter was in the sky must be very good. I've just received today 4 copies of my book called JOBBER SKALD (which was called 'Weymouth Sands' in America) it is translated into Italian and Published in Milan. It has part of a picture by Derain in bold blues and reds of ships at Tower bridge somehow printed on the actual cover which looks very fine. I hope your burglars are still too scared of your witchcraft to meddle with your room.

Yours faithfully ever and always. John Cowper Powys

[*Purdy to Powys 34*]
236 Henry Street, Brooklyn 1, New York,
July 19, 1962

My dear Friend,

Orion has long since disappeared from the skies, and I have been studying Ophiuchus, the Serpent-Holder, mentioned in Milton in <u>Paradise Lost</u>, and am also gazing at Jupiter and Saturn after midnight, and at Venus at sunset.

I am trying to finish my new novel about the Brooklyn rapist, titled

CABOT WRIGHT BEGINS. I had a nice letter from Dame Edith, but she alas is not feeling too well owing to a slipped disk in her spine ... we are having a very queer summer, it is very cool in July – unheard of! I did run off to Nantucket island for a few days, to see what Herman Melville may have seen there; but it is a place for wealthy dowagers and spoiled rich people, and I had to return. How Are you, my dear friend, and what are you doing? with affectionate wishes from your friend, ever, Jim

1963 Purdy to Powys 35

[*Purdy to Powys 35*]
236 Henry Street, Brooklyn 1, New York USA
February 26, 1963

MY DEAR JACK,

How are you? I think of you very often, and wish I lived close so I could visit you when you would be in the mood for company.

My Mother died on December 14, and I was in Ohio. I was heartbroken. I am very alone now in the world.

I am trying to finish my new novel CABOT WRIGHT BEGINS, concerning a Brooklyn rapist. I am also writing a one-act play about a Negress who murdered her 6 husbands, named TECMESSA STARR. Dame Edith is coming into American waters, on May 8, in Port Everglades, Florida, and has asked me to come to see her. If I can get some money together, I might.

How is Miss Playter? And Blaenau's Malcolm? Do you walk with the magic cane at all?

Do write me,

Your friend who sends Love to you and Miss Playter,

   Ever, Jim   James Purdy.

John Cowper Powys died on 17 June 1963; Dame Edith Sitwell died on 9 December 1964.

NOTES

1. Not *63: Dream Palace* (see next letter) but the privately-printed *Don't Call Me by My Right Name and other stories* (1956), a copy of which Purdy had also sent to Edith Sitwell. All the stories in this volume are included in *Color of Darkness*, with two added stories as well as '63: Dream Palace'.
2. Allentown and Scranton, both in Pennsylvania, had large Welsh-speaking communities, of miners seeking work outside of Wales; they were served by at least two newspapers, *The Druid* and *The Welsh American*.
3. Victor Gollancz (1893-1967), influential publisher and radical reformer.
4. Enid Starkie (1897-1970), Fellow of Somerville College, Oxford, Reader in French and biographer of Rimbaud, Flaubert and others.
5. On Phyllis Paul see Glen Cavaliero, *The Supernatural in English Fiction* (Oxford UP 1995), which relates Paul's fiction to the range of supernatural elements in Powys's novels; see also Cavaliero's introduction to Phyllis Paul, *A Cage for the Nightingale* (Sundial, 2012). Elizabeth Bowen praised Paul's fiction as 'unforgettable and strange'.
6. *La Celestina* (1499), a play by Fernando de Rojas that inaugurates the literary renaissance in Spain.
7. Mary Norton (1903-92), *The Borrowers*, illustrated by Diane Stanley, 1952; a sequel *The Borrowers Afield* was published in 1955. These tales of characters who live underground delighted John Cowper; for the influence on Powys of children's literature see Richard Maxwell, *The Historical Novel in Europe* (Cambridge UP, 2009), 264-6.
8. The offending word: 'motherfucker'.
9. Meifod is Montgomeryshire; 'Maen' means 'stone'; Rhodric Mawr (c.820-878), ruler of Gwynedd from 844, and also of Powys from 855.
10. Presumably taken by Carl Van Vechten (1880-1964), acknowledged as a photographer of Greenwich Village life and of the Harlem Renaissance; in 1956-58 Van Vechten made a number of portraits of Purdy, one of which is reproduced as the frontispiece to this volume.
11. Glyn Jones (1905-1955) was a Welsh poet, novelist and critic, and a friend of Powys, who did translate Welsh literature though not the *Mabinogion*. Gwyn Jones (1907-99) translated the *Mabinogion*, with Thomas Jones, in 1948, for Dent's Everyman series.
12. Charlotte Guest (1812-95) completed her translation of the *Mabinogion* in 1849. She was the daughter of the Earl of Lindsey and her maiden name was Bertie; her second husband, Charles Schreiber (1826-84), was not German but English, and served as MP for Poole; Lady Charlotte Schreiber's collection of china is not at the British Museum but at the Victoria & Albert.
13. Carl Van Vechten (1880-1964) photographer, writer, patron of the Harlem

Renaissance, the literary executor of Gertrude Stein and promoter of Langston Hughes and Richard Wright.
14 Gamel Woolsey (1897-1968), poet and novelist, born in South Carolina, married Gerald Brenan (1894-1987).
15 Purdy's story 'About Jessie Mae' was published in the *New Yorker* of 25 May 1957, and subsequently included in Purdy's *Children Is All* (New Directions, 1962).
16 The publication of Purdy's early work is bibliographically complex: what New Directions published as *Color of Darkness: eleven stories and a novella* on 4 December 1957 (see Purdy to Powys 12 and Powys to Purdy 30) had already been published in July by Gollancz — the contents identical — under the title *63: Dream Palace*. In 1961 this volume — with the addition of Dame Edith's Preface — would be issued again in London, this time by Secker and Warburg, as *Colour of Darkness*.
17 Powys's letter in the *Observer* of 14 July 1957 refers to Sappho, Shakespeare, Aristophanes and Dante as writers who had dared to deal with homoerotic themes.
18 The lines in Greek letters are from *Iliad* 15. 286-88: 'Now look you, verily a great marvel is this that mine eyes behold, how that now he is risen again and hath avoided the fates ...'
19 John Masefield, born 1878, was Poet Laureate from 1930 until his death in 1967.
20 The 1956 film adaptation of *Moby Dick* by John Huston, script by Ray Bradbury, starring Gregory Peck and Leo Genn; parts were filmed in Wales.
21 Harry Coombes's critical study *T.F. Powys* was published by Barrie and Rockliff in 1960.
22 Jacques in *As You Like It*, Act 2 Scene vii.
23 Alejo Carpentier (1904-1980), Cuban writer and pioneer of 'magic realism'; *El Reino de Este Mundo* was published in 1949.
24 The Sesame Club, Edith Sitwell's London base for many years, had been founded in 1895 for professional women; see 'Lady Natasha Spender remembers Edith Sitwell', *Daily Telegraph*, 8 June 2008.
25 Stillman's Gym, founded in 1911 in Brooklyn, was famous as an arena for prize fights; it was the setting for the 1956 film about Rocky Graziano, 'Somebody Up There Likes Me' with Paul Newman.
26 *Peter Whiffle: his life and works*, a fictionalized memoir by Carl Van Vechten published by Knopf in 1922.
27 *The Color of Darkness* was translated by Helen Hentze as *Die Farbe der Dunkelheit: Elf Stories und eine Novelle*. Hamburg: Rowohlt Verlag, 1959. There was to be no Swedish translation, though in 1963 Bonnier did publish *Brorsonen*, Håkan Norlén's translation of *The Nephew*. The editors have had recourse to Rainer J. Hanshe's 'James Purdy Bibliography' published in *Hyperion: a web publication of The Nietzsche Circle*, Vol. VI, no. 1 (March 2011), 206-28.
28 The first of Purdy's books to be published in Spain was *Color de Oscuridad: once relatos y un cuento*. Barcelona: Seix Barral, 1963. *El Sobrino* (The Nephew) had been

published in Buenos Aires in 1962.

29 Paul Swan (1884-1972) was a sculptor, painter and dancer; known as 'the most beautiful man in the world' he would have been 73 when Purdy saw him. A portraitist of famous people including Isadora Duncan, Willa Cather, Maurice Ravel, Charles Lindberg, Presidents Roosevelt and Kennedy, and Pope Paul VI, he was himself the subject of an Andy Warhol film in 1965. Raymond Duncan (1874-1966), dancer, artist, poet, and brother of Isadora.

30 Not from 'Ulalume' but from Poe's 'The Conqueror Worm', somewhat loosely recollected.

31 In the chapter 'Consummation'.

32 *Color of darkness: eleven stories and a novella,* New York: New Directions, 1957.

33 *Double Exposure*, translated from the French by Elisabeth Abbott, Vanguard Press, New York, 1956. A comic treatment of an ordinary working man who is 'possessed' by a hero of the Napoleonic Wars, Baron Tailliard, this account of an 'invasion' of reality by the past would have obvious appeal to Powys, though no serious writer is likely to feel honoured by the comparison he makes. Théo Fleischman (1893-1979) was a much decorated Belgian war hero as well as a pioneer, from 1926, of news-broadcasting.

34 The New Directions edition of *Color of Darkness: eleven stories and a novella.*

35 David Brynley (1902-81) and Norman Notley (c.1890-1980) were vocalists who specialized in the repertoire of Elizabethan song and the Baroque. Brynley was born in Wales; Notley taught in Canada, at McGill University, during the First War. With the New English Singers, founded in 1932, and on their own, they toured in North America before 1939; they were based in the U.S. from 1945 until 1970 when they retired to England, living in Corfe Castle. See Christopher Le Fleming, *Journey into Music (by the Slow Train)*. Bristol: Redcliffe, 1982.

36 Otherwise known as Gerrit Dou (1613-1675).

37 The film 'Cowboy' (1958) is based not on Frank Harris's *My Life and Loves* but on *My Reminiscences as a Cowboy* (1930).

38 Marguerite Allotte de la Fuy's biography of her uncle, *Jules Verne, sa vie, son oeuvre.* Paris: Simon Kra, 1928; the English translation was published by Staples Press in 1954.

39 H. Richard Archer (1911-1978) moved in 1957 to the Chapin Library at Williams College, Williamstown, Massachusetts (not Pennsylvania) and later became its Director. (Thanks to Larry Mitchell for this information).

40 Alluding to the nursery rhyme: The Man in the moon came tumbling down/ And asked the way to Norwich/ He went by the South, and burnt his mouth/ With eating cold pease porridge.

41 *Letters of John Cowper Powys to Louis Wilkinson 1935-1956.* London: Macdonald, 1958.

CORRESPONDENCE

[42] The *Kalevala* is the national epic of Finland, compiled by Elias Lönnrot from Finnish and Karelian folklore and mythology, and first published in its entirety in 1849 — the same year in which Lady Charlotte Guest completed her translation of the *Mabinogion*.

[43] *Malcolm* would be published by Farrar, Straus, & Cudahy.

[44] Giangiacomo Feltrinelli (1926-72) founded the publishing house in 1954; many of Purdy's books were translated into Italian though all were published by Einaudi, not Feltrinelli.

[45] Osbert Sitwell (1892-1969).

[46] *Commentary*, a journal whose contributors included Lionel Trilling, Irving Howe, Daniel Bell and Hannah Arendt. Founded in 1945, it was edited by Elliot Cohen until 1960; thereafter, until 1995, by Norman Podhoretz.

[47] *Encore Theatre Magazine*, based in London, ran from 1954 to 1965.

[48] Lynn Caine (1924-1987) was Director of Publicity at Farrar, Straus until 1967 when she joined Little, Brown; she is best known for her memoir *Widow* (1974).

[49] This last sentence was subsequently quoted on the jacket of *Malcolm*, along with commendations by Dorothy Parker and Lillian Hellman.

[50] Dorothy Parker had written an appreciation of *Malcolm* in *Esquire Magazine*: 'a prodigiously funny book' whose author is 'a writer of the highest rank in originality and insight'.

[51] Angus Wilson (1913-1991) was a consistent admirer of John Cowper Powys as well as a defender of Purdy. He promoted the publication of *Malcolm* by Secker and Warburg (Wilson's own publisher), and came to Purdy's defence after the publication of *Eustace Chisholm and the Works* (1967), a novel now highly regarded and often re-issued as a gay classic. By 1967 Purdy could no longer rely on support from Powys or Edith Sitwell, but Wilson came to his defence. The London publisher of *Eustace Chisholm* was not Secker (to whom Wilson remained always loyal) but Jonathan Cape.

[52] The Guggenheim Museum, designed by Frank Lloyd Wright, was commissioned in 1943 though not opened until 1959.

[53] Robert Giroux (1914-2008), one of the most celebrated publishers of modern literature, joined Farrar, Straus, & Cudahy in 1955; the firm was later named Farrar, Straus, and Giroux.

[54] This suggests that Giroux had tried to interest American publishers in Powys; any such attempt has yet to be documented.

[55] *Malcolm* was translated into Danish by Elsa Gress Wright and published by Arena Forfatternes in 1962; the same firm had already published Wright's translations of *63: Dream Palace* (*63, drømmeslottet*, 1960) and *The Nephew* (*Nevøen*, 1961).

[56] *The Nephew* is 'Dedicated to John Cowper Powys and Robert Giroux'.

[57] James Laughlin (1914-97), founder of New Directions and disciple of Ezra Pound

[58] New Directions never re-issued any books by Powys.
[58] *A Skeleton Key to Finnegans Wake* by Joseph Campbell and Henry Morton Robinson. NY: Harcourt, Brace, 1944.
[59] Citing Chapter 38 of Gibbon's *Decline and Fall of the Roman Empire*.
[60] Gallimard published *Malcolm* in Marie Canavaggia's French translation in 1961.
[61] 'Mush' is a dish made from cornmeal.
[62] President Eisenhower led a Peace Tour to South America from February 23 to March 7 1960.
[63] Powys confuses *Weymouth Sands* (first published in Britain as *Jobber Skald*) with his first published novel, *Wood and Stone*.
[64] John Redwood Anderson (1883-1964), poet, had been a neighbour of Powys in Corwen, North Wales: see Powys to Purdy 19.
[65] J. & E. Bumpus Ltd. of Oxford Street was a long-established and respected London bookshop; see Purdy to Powys 16.
[66] Gilbert Highet (1906-1978), British classical scholar appointed in 1938 as Professor of Latin & Greek at Columbia University, New York; Powys's gift to Purdy was Highet's *Poets in a Landscape* (1957); see Powys to Purdy 59.
[67] Marie Canavaggia's translation of *Autobiography* (*Autobiographie*) would be published by Gallimard in 1965.
[68] Napier Wilt (1896-1975), Professor of English at the University of Chicago and Dean of Humanities from 1951 until his retirement in 1962. Specialist in history of theatre in Chicago; published articles on Edgar Allen Poe and Ambrose Bierce and a volume on American Humour. His admiration for Powys is undocumented.

JONATHAN GOODWIN

Animated Fictions: Characters in *The Brazen Head*

Even by John Cowper Powys's impressive standard, *The Brazen Head* is a difficult and puzzling work. Inspired by reading his fellow anti-vivisectionist Evalyn Westacott's book on Roger Bacon (Krissdóttir 406), *The Brazen Head* is set in Wessex in the first half of 1272. Though the familiar legend of Bacon's talking bronze head motivates some of the plot, equal attention is paid to the supernatural magnetic exercises of Peter Peregrinus, who imagines himself to be the anti-Christ. Bonaventura also makes an appearance as a fanatic tormented by repressed sexual urges, and at the end it is Albertus Magnus who appears to reconcile opposites. Less well-attested personages include several baronial families, and two important Jewish characters: Peleg, a Mongolian giant, and Ghosta, a young woman who enchants Bacon's brazen head and eventually marries Peleg.

To describe how these various arrangements of personalities generate the plot of *The Brazen Head*, I draw on Alex Woloch's definition of character-system: 'the arrangement of multiple and differentiated character-spaces — differentiated configurations and manipulations of the human figure — into a unified narrative structure.'[1] Woloch describes 'character-spaces' as the encounter between a human personality and the 'determined space and position within the narrative as a whole' (Woloch 14). I propose to read *The Brazen Head* through this concept of character-system and character-spaces. In so doing, I aim to explain some of the problems identified by Peter G. Christensen as 'frustrated narration'. In particular, Christensen argues that the narrator has no explanation for the causes of many of the events, or that he proposes many incompatible explanations; this creates a sense of frustration and thwarted understanding, not least in the reader. (Christensen 'Frustrated' 96)

This sense of frustration may be clarified if we take into account the narrator's unusual notions about animated thoughts, or *eidola*, and see how they operate within Powys's character-system. The manner in which Ghosta brings the brazen head to life is perhaps the strangest incident in a novel filled with the improbable and the stupendous. (I refer to the text as a 'novel' as a generic shorthand; 'historical romance' might be more precise, though each of Powys's fictions might best be regarded as *sui generis*.) A shared thought or desire has brought Ghosta to the castle where Roger Bacon is a prisoner, and eventually to his room. Bacon himself had wondered if the only thing that his automaton was lacking was the *secretum secretorum* which could be found only in a virginal womb. (In the novel Bacon refers to a medieval manuscript attributed to Aristotle called the *Secretum Secretorum*, 'secret of secrets'. This text — which is not fictional — does not in fact have any of the occultist associations Powys ascribes to it.) Bacon and his servant, Brother Tuck, encourage the willing Ghosta to straddle the brazen head and rub her genitals against its face. She later confesses to Peleg that she felt great sexual pleasure in doing this, though the entire event has been described with great solemnity.

This tension between solemnity and eros characterizes the narrative. Scenes with a strong erotic component are described in a strangely detached, perhaps humorous mode. The first such scene shows Lil-Umbra, the daughter of one of the local barons, watching the sunrise with the giant Peleg. They are sitting together in a familiar alcove; their thoughts and actions are suggestive. The effect is heightened by Peleg's exotic physical appearance and apparently stimulating philosophizing. Peleg and Lil-Umbra can see both the moon and the sun at once, and Peleg develops a theory of 'double opposites' based on this image:

> 'Take ourselves. Take me for example. The first of my two Opposites is in myself, that is to say, my greedy-grasping body on one side and my obedient, faithful and well-behaved soul on the other side. But the second of my two Opposites is my whole self, body and soul together, as opposed to the entire Creation or the total universe of which I am a living part.' (*The Brazen Head* [henceforth *BH*] 19)

In addition to these 'double oppositions' a parallel opposition exists between the petite young English girl Lil-Umbra and the Mongolian giant. The entire notion of opposites attracting and eroticism being generated by their unknown (and culturally forbidden) attraction occurs throughout Powys's work. Morine Krissdóttir has called attention to the prevalence of voyeurism in Powys's fiction (Krissdóttir 67), and the 'chronicler' (as the narrator of the book refers to himself on several occasions) shows an obviously prurient interest which, in this scene and elsewhere, infects and distorts both his descriptions and his representations of the characters' conversation. Thus oppositions and parallels become distorted and refracted in the telling, and the reader needs to work to find the pattern and the structure.

The doctrine of double opposites owes something to Bacon's own theories, and Peleg significantly acquires his knowledge of these philosophies from within, rather than deriving them directly from Bacon or his writings. Here is a relatively mild example of the anachronism that permeates the book. The type of anachronism that interests me is chiefly of the linguistic and conceptual variety. Anachronism itself is a subject of much theoretical interest in the study of the historical novel. Georg Lukács pointed out the 'necessary anachronism' of the historical novel (Lukács 156), by which the present would always infect even the most scrupulous recreation of the past. As a general historicist insight, this claim is hard to dispute, but Lukács recognized, as have many critics since, that some historical novelists try much harder than others to eliminate anachronistic features and aspects.[2]

Powys is not one of those who try hard to eliminate anachronisms. Peter G. Christensen, in a study of the historical context of *The Brazen Head*, notes that 'we are not in the world of Sir Walter Scott, enshrined forever by Georg Lukács'.(Christensen 'Wessex' 35) One immediate explanation is that Powys is writing a form of romance which has no expectation of material or conceptual accuracy. Another would extend the romance to a type of personalized psychological projection where each character represents an urge or philosophical concept in Powys's own character-system, which is only loosely tied to the era in which the fiction is set. *The Brazen Head* presents evidence for both of these explanations. The narrator will often make self-referential comments about the 'chronicler's duty', and the general tendency of these comments impresses upon the reader an awareness of the lack of historical accuracy in the events and characters. None of the characters behaves, after all, in a manner that could be even approximately attributed to any of them from the available historical documentation.

Along with the relative unimportance of historical accuracy (or the acceptance of anachronisms), the second distinguishing feature of the book is its uncertain and meandering plotting. Here is a quality that *The Brazen Head* does not share with the romance genre in particular. Krissdóttir notes that Powys reported frustration during the composition of the book, itself quite rapid, over a few months: 'He felt that his mind was "disintegrating in so many ways at once that I find it hard to steer it in the direction I desire to go".' (Krissdóttir 410) She also reports that he benefited from the assistance of Phyllis Playter, who gave him 'wonderful help in the difficult business of connecting the characters with the plot of the story.' (Krissdóttir 410)[3] The plot very much reads as if these connections were a source of struggle for the author. Peter Peregrinus, for instance, seems to be clearly the antagonist, yet he remains out of our view for more than two-thirds of the book.

There are several explanations for this confused narrative structure. One is that confusion may be only apparent, a cunning device to prevent us from too easily detecting the structure. Most of Powys's other works ramble, however, and he seldom reported the kind of trouble he had resolving them as he did with *The Brazen Head*. Another explanation is that Powys found himself incapable of resolving the plot, and that its apparent confusedness is actual, a sign of some sort of failure. A third, and perhaps more satisfactory explanation, is that it is anachronism itself that accounts for the apparent confusion. The logic of the narrative is not typical of the historical novel or even of the romance, but may be the reflection of the dream-logic of unconscious desires. Frequent asides and commentaries seem to recognize and endorse this interpretation. For example: 'What the lady thus addressed felt in her secret mind, as she listened to this fantastic progeny of the King of Bohemia, it would be impossible for a male chronicler to describe' (*BH* 32). This may be only a coy demurral, not out of place in many narratives. But when Powys describes another of Bacon's inventions that had the power to broadcast the thoughts of a third person, a more dubious discourse emerges:

> For Brother Tuck wondered how soon Prior Bog would detect something amiss if he, Tuck of Abbotsbury, fried his own excrement for the Priory supper; and Roger of Ilchester wondered whether it would be possible for a female yellow-hammer to lay eggs if she were impregnated by a dead mate who had been galvanized into momentary sexual excitement by a thunderstorm. (*BH* 89)

Here the chronicler abandons the pretence of having omniscient access to the characters' thoughts; instead he ascribes to them some of his own fancies and concerns. The point of these is not to show, as the explanation purports to do, what odd thoughts will pass through the minds of otherwise occupied and normal people, but to call attention to how strange and non-realistic the entire fiction is. By explicit contrast, Powys takes pains to highlight what he views as Bacon's 'ordinary' Englishness and sound practical sense. The chronicler's words remind the reader that this is far from a straightforward updating of a legend about medieval magicians, and certainly not one that 'explains' the marvellous in a realistic mode. The ordinariness of these medieval lives is transformed in the modern re-telling to a fantasy or a romance that would have tested the credibility of any medieval audience.

Powys further departs from the generic conventions of the chronicle or romance through the multitude and relative importance of the minor characters. Roger Bacon and Peter Peregrinus are the plot's major characters, but it is the brazen head that brings all of them together, in all their diversity. Spardo, the bastard son of the King of Bohemia, for instance, seems invested with great significance in his description and the access given to his thoughts, but the plot does little to redeem this special attention. Similarly, his horse Cheiron, which is likened to the mythical centaur because of a tumor on his neck which impresses several of the characters as an embryonic or emerging human head, has one significant scene. Yet this scene quite fails to match up to the apparently mythical importance ascribed to Cheiron.

Alex Woloch describes two different approaches to minor characters, as exemplified respectively by Dickens and Balzac: 'Dickens's panoply of eccentrics and grotesques brings minor characters to the centre of his novels by increasing their distortion. Balzac, in an attempt to give every character potential roundness, bursts apart the seams of *La Comédie Humaine*, creating one vast and interconnected narrative universe.' (Woloch 35) At first glance, Powys's method would seem Dickensian, but the chronicler's tendency to wander, and to invest each character's thoughts with apparently undue significance and gravity, suggests a more Balzacian approach. Woloch's concept of character-distortion lends itself to the treatment of Powys's method. His minor characters certainly tend toward the grotesque, and aspects of their personality are clearly exaggerated in order to make them fit into the novel's conceptual scheme, or ideological nexus. Dod Pole's labour rebellion is one example of something that emerges quite unexpectedly from a character-space rather less distorted than the reader might expect.

At the same time, however, the lack of clearly defined major characters in *The Brazen Head* (or in the far larger work, *A Glastonbury Romance*) means that the minor characters receive something close to central description in the novel's character-system. And there are parallels between the characters. The opposition between Peter Peregrinus and Roger Bacon[4] extends to others: Spardo and Peleg, Lilith and Lil-Umbra. This last opposition is intriguing to consider because of their competing erotic styles: Lil-Umbra is a healthy ingenue about whom Bonaventura spreads rumours of incest, while Lilith is a temptress modelled after Salomé. Lilith seduces Bonaventura and forces him to engage in a reaction-formation against Bacon and his presumed supporters, with Lil-Umbra receiving the brunt of Bonaventura's own horror of sexuality. The opposition between Spardo and Peleg is more subtle: the wandering man-at-arms (or 'knight-errant') and bastard son of the King of Bohemia, Spardo is a man of action who distrusts the machinations of the intellect, whereas Peleg, an intellectual in exile — and a giant — is also a man of action, yet one who spends much of his time in contemplation.

It requires both Peleg and Spardo to protect the head of brass. Among the most intriguing of the characters' oppositions is the way in which Bacon and Peregrinus respectively employ the *energeia akinesis*. Powys glosses this phrase — which also occurs in *In Defence of Sensuality* (56, 143), *Up and Out* (214), and *Porius* (646) — as 'energy without fuss' (*BH* 251). It is the 'self-creative energy' (Krissdóttir 410) which allows Ghosta to breathe life into the brazen head and which gives Peregrinus power focused through a phallus-like magnet that he keeps close to his own genitals. Ghosta's fascination with the concept of parthenogenesis explains why she agrees to perform this intimate act in front of witnesses, and it seems that she feels that her interest in it has all along been the *energeia akinesis* acting through her. The phallic destructiveness of Peregrinus, and his exercise of animal magnetism, is a concentration of pure force. He desires nothing less than to impose himself upon the world, and his aggressivity is a parody of male sexuality.

What Powys slyly invites the reader to consider is that the concept of *energeia akinesis* — invoked by the chronicler himself in order to explain these narrative motivations — is itself an explanation of his writing method. It is not so much an element within the plot as a self-reflective indication of its own compositional method. *The energeia akinesis*, being without fuss or form, purely potential rather than actualized (or kinetic) energy, is therefore timeless. This concern with timelessness features prominently throughout Powys's writing, and becomes the dominant theme of *The Brazen Head*.

The theme culminates, of course, in the destruction of the brazen head the moment before it completes its litany about time. The phrase 'time will be' remains forever unuttered. Such an ending could be read as either apocalyptic or merely coy. The self-contained universe of this fictional world will know no time but its own, as activated by the reader's imagination, and it will never enter into the time to come — the actual historical time in which we are reading the novel. The oracle is thus disrupted, and the oracle's broken utterance confines the brazen head to the world in which its story is told, excluding it from the world in which it's read. The erection of the brass wall around England to protect it from invasion, a part of the legend that caught the attention of writers such as Shelley and Carlyle, is not even mentioned in *The Brazen Head*. A boundary imposed on time renders quite redundant any barrier in space.

The idea of *The Brazen Head* as a mapping — or a telling — of Powys's own notions of time and space, of matter and its animation, could explain much of the unreality and lack of specificity in its historical setting. But there are some plot-related matters for which this notion does not adequately account. What is to be made of the denizens of the Lost Towers, for example, or of Lady Lilt's strong commitment to vegetarianism? Krissdóttir notes that Powys was quite open about peopling his novels with characters drawn from his own life, and, more importantly, from his own obsessions. The anti-vivisectionist movement strongly correlates with vegetarianism, and in this respect the novel is indebted to Evalyn Westacott.[5] When Baron Maldung longs to eat a rabbit, Lady Lilt forces him to go out in the woods and apologize to the plants before she will sleep with him again. Their daughter Lilith's seeming perversity might be thought to derive from these unorthodox ideas, but the positive presentation of her eroticism could also indicate sympathy. Much remains unclear.

I have argued that Lilith is meant to be a counterpart to Lil-Umbra, whose apparent virginity and love for the courtly Raymond de Laon is itself undermined by her own strong will and her erotic conversations with Peleg. Lilith and her family exhibit such an exaggerated Gothic sensibility that Glen Cavaliero notes that they 'seem to have wandered straight off the drawing-board of Charles Addams'. (Cavaliero 142) And their House-of-Usher style mutual destruction of themselves and the Brazen Head at the end (along with Peter Peregrinus) is what saves the time of the novel from the time-destroying magic of the lodestone and the brazen head.[6] The fiction often feels apocalyptic, and the dialectic interplay between the characters shows how the balance of their respective mystical and ideological forces prevents any of their apocalyptic desires from influencing history, let alone transforming it. But there is a paradox here in that the setting itself is radically ahistorical and thus 'unreal'.[7] From the perspective of the setting, the apocalypse that the characters seek would be a breakthrough from the realm of potential energy and fictionality into that of kinetic energy and actuality. The transvalued world that Peregrinus seeks to create is, for Powys, much closer to the historical actuality than the fiction Powys has placed him in. Similarly, Lilith is a sex-fantasy object, one who comes tantalizingly close to being actualized, and whose meteoric apotheosis is an attempt to reach into lived experience.

Such a hypothesis may seem highly conjectural, yet the evidence of Powys's correspondence supports such an interpretation, and permits even stranger ones. For example, in a letter to Nicholas Ross of 19 February 1955: 'My romance centres round far the most important figure of the Middle Ages, namely ROGER BACON who succeeded in doing what no other human being has ever done before or since. That is to say Friar Roger Bacon, who was infinitely greater than Francis Bacon, imitated God and created a living Soul!' (*Letters to Ross*, 127) This passage may suggest that Powys believed that Bacon actually invented a brazen head, though it is hard to imagine what sources he could have found to support this interpretation. It is more likely that Powys embraced what he saw as the larger symbolic truth of the legendary powers ascribed to Bacon. He was thinking of Bacon not as a historical figure but as one within the larger conceptual scheme of his 'character-system'. On 7 May 1954 Powys had told Louis Wilkinson that he had consulted Scott for his meticulousness with period detail (*Letters to Wilkinson*, 307-8), while indicating that he would be working in the romance mode. His last fictions remove themselves even further from the depiction of a recognizable reality and move into the fantastic. While it would be possible to read *The Brazen Head* as a transitional text from historical to fantastic fictions it would be better to insist that Powys's historical fiction was always deeply inflected by the fantastic.

There are various possible generic descriptions of *The Brazen Head* — historical novel, fantasy, romance, chronicle — but none is decisively apt. Brebner points out several inconsistencies in plotting and descriptions (apart from the obvious historical inaccuracies and anachronisms): Peter Peregrinus's personality varies widely between different chapters and his lodestone fetish is described as being of different lengths, though all within the bounds of phallic possibility. (Brebner 219) A generous interpretation of Peregrinus's inconsistent character-spaces is that his journey in the 'symbolic wasteland' is a spiritual one, and that his character there may reflect its multiple essences — his whole malevolence, in other words, as distinct from the mask he displays to the people he meets. The enactment of thought, either of an individual personality or through collective willing, is one of Powys's enduring concerns. He constantly returns to the *eidola*, animated images of thought, or a reservoir of emotion. The word 'eidolon' was (according to the *OED*) first used in English by Carlyle and Scott, both of whom share Powys's interest in anachronism and the larger problems of historical understanding. The concept of the eidolon can help us to elucidate *The Brazen Head*'s generic peculiarities.

Ghosta, the young Jewish woman, feels a very strong affinity for the concept of the Holy Ghost. A ghost can be a vestige of a strong emotion or personality. The eidolon is for Powys a thought giving birth to an animate enmity. Ghosta is deeply interested in parthenogenesis.[8] She gives birth to the Brazen Head and animates it through carnal contact. Ghosta is thus the point of contact between two worlds: the fictive and the real, the potential and the kinetic. What she bears will eventually be destroyed, and history will return to its 'normal' state. All fictional characters are in some sense like eidola, but in *The Brazen Head* Powys's create their own. They recognize and feel affinities for persons who are related to them only in the character-system of their creator. A passage that illustrates this dynamic occurs early in the book in the encounter between Lil-Umbra and the Bailiff Heger Syberius:

> Indeed they both felt in a weird and rather frightening manner that between the two of them, on this special day of this special month of the year of grace twelve hundred and seventy-two, an extremely formidable thought-child had been born, a thought-child, or rather a fate-child, for whose growth in power and for whose increase in stature a moment was as a day and a day was as a year; so that before a few months were over something would happen that would make their coming together on this particular morning a fearful and memorable milestone, not merely in the history of Roque Manor but in the history of the planet Earth. (*BH* 68)

One significance of the year 1272 for Powys was that it was six hundred years before his own birth.[9] While the thought-child or fate-child referred to in this paragraph would seem to be the brazen head, it also implies the concept of a temporal loop in which the events set in motion give birth to the author six hundred years hence, who then imaginatively recreates these historical circumstances. It might seem far-fetched to imagine that the destruction of the brazen head would be a proximate cause of the birth of John Cowper Powys in Derbyshire, but it is not far-fetched to suppose that the modern world itself would not have come into being without the creation and destruction of Roger Bacon's oracular device. Ghosta, who gives symbolic birth to the brazen head, is a mature synthesis of the virginal Lil-Umbra and the sexual obsessive Lilith. The desires that bring Ghosta to Bacon to give birth to the head, and that cause Ghosta to confront one of her sublated stages in Lilith, themselves issue from the thought-child formed by the meeting of Lil-Umbra and Heger Syberius in the armoury.

As I have observed of eidola in *A Glastonbury Romance*: 'thoughts become eidola and impose themselves upon the fictive reality. Powys thought that this fictive reality imposes itself upon him or any writer who considers the nature of social being or who merely thinks about the world around him'. (Goodwin 116) If the concept of *eidola* is the main motivating factor of the text, then the novel's apparent plotlessness and other formal difficulties can be more easily explained. The romance as a genre does not tend to be plotless, yet Cavaliero notes that *The Brazen Head* has almost none. (Cavaliero 141) Powys's apparent lack of plotting might be better explained as a formal necessity.

It is eidola that make visible this apparent chaos. And they give us a peculiar version of character. Debates in literary theory about character have, in broad terms, alternated between evaluating them either morally as persons or formally as structural features. In *The Brazen Head*, precisely for the reasons we have explored, these two poles are indistinguishable. For example, when Heber Sygerius and Lil-Umbra both apprehend the eidolon of Ghosta, they become aware of her importance in the plot's symbolic economy. Ghosta has only a structural relation to Lil-Umbra (and to Sygerius through her). The image of Ghosta is more than a mental perception; it reveals to Lil-Umbra what she will become. While Lil-Umbra's effect on Peleg awakens his sensitivity to Ghosta, Heber Sygerius's quite non-paternal interest in her as an erotic being makes Lil-Umbra sensitive to Ghosta as a premonition of her own future.

If further proof of the dialectic generation of character-spaces were needed, Peleg provides it. He has had a similar role to Heber

Sygerius and will be drawn to Ghosta once she appears to him. When Peleg and Sygerius meet, we are told that the flame of the fire in the armoury becomes somehow aware of their unconscious thoughts and desires, desires that are called 'sub-sexual' (*BH* 73). I am tempted to claim that Sygerius's speech about the Four Gods makes sense only in terms of the novel's antithetical structure. The Four Gods are those of logical opposition. Each concept has both a contrary and a contradiction, and each of Powys's characters is itself a concept: the contraries and oppositions are quite blatant.

Also revealing of how the book might be read is the restrained way in which violence is described. There are a number of violent scenes, which is of course consistent with Powys's lifelong interest in violence and sadism, and these scenes invite interpretation in terms of personal allegory. Yet they are thick with the 'circumambient metaphysics' that Glen Cavaliero has identified: he refers specifically to the scene in Peleg's cave where the Horm's omnipresence is described, though their threat of violence is strangely muted (*BH* 143). The scene in which Baron Maldung shoots an arrow at Baron Boncor, apparently spurred on in some vague fashion by the sexual desires of his daughter Lilith, is also notably circumspect. The battle over the brazen head between the forces loyal to the King and those loyal to Bonaventura, though filled with violent action, produces only one truly violent description, and that is apparently marginal: of the accidental death of a badger cub.

Peter Peregrinus is the active principle of violence in the novel, whereas Peleg is its passive agent. Though Peleg is capable of great violence, drawing on his own energy, he remains inwardly peaceful while Peregrinus is filled with an inner rage which he directs outwards into violence through the use of his lodestone. The symbolic aspects of the lodestone are seldom more apparent than when Peter treats it as the agent of his will; he can even project an act of violence into the future, as when he 'brings about' the future murder of Edward II. When John, Lil-Umbra's brother, is tormented by sadistic fantasies involving rape by fiery rods and other objects, one source of those fantasies seems to be Peregrinus's lodestone. However, John puts these violent fantasies to creative purposes. Unlike others, John is able to cope with the fecundity of his imagination, even when stimulated by eidola projected from outside. Powys would straightforwardly claim in *All or Nothing* that masturbation was superior to fornication because it created something out of images alone. (Brebner 282) Just as Peleg's fantasy of smashing skulls with his huge mace prefigures and inverts his defence of the brazen head, John's fantasies of rape by foreign objects is figured by his own sculpture of the Virgin; Peregrinus or Bonaventura also fantasize about animating this sculpture, just as Bacon has animated the brazen head.

The central motive of the novel is, as I have argued, the animating power of fantasy. Bacon uses this power mechanically and engineers an oracular object. The characters in the story become aware that they are 'animated fictions' set in schematic opposition to one another. Each of them transforms this recognition into a metaphysical justification of their desires and drives. An early instance occurs when Lady Val is thinking of her husband Sir Mort's idea of the invisible panpsychic dimension:

> His theory culminated in the amazing dogma that everything that existed had such feelings, not even excluding rocks and stones and earth-mould. And he further held that this invisible Dimension was much more crowded and much more active at certain geographical points round the surface of land and water than at others. Even where there are no human beings, this spiritual atmosphere would, he maintained, be there just the same. For not only must there be, universally emanating from the whole body of our planet, feelings that we must think of as the feelings of our Mother

> the Earth herself, but there must also be the feelings — or semi-conscious vibrations corresponding to feelings — of all the separate material elements whereof the substance of the planet is composed. (*BH* 165)

There are spatial reservoirs of this hidden dimension of feeling in most of Powys's fiction, and this is often where characters realize their own status within the character-system. The 'invisible Dimension' is thus a self-conscious artifact of literary creation, not a claim about actuality, whether historical, extra-fictional or metaphysical. Nor should it raise questions of belief or the suspension of disbelief. The 'separate material elements' may recall alchemy and Westacott's alchemical history of Roger Bacon — Powys's immediate inspiration — yet here they 'merely' structure and give narrative shape to fictional worlds and character-spaces. Physical landmarks are imbued with special significance by fictional characters who are thus led to recognize, through the *shared* attribution of an animating spirit, the role of the *deus absconditus* author in their own narrative. It is precisely this, I suggest, that motivates a great deal of their otherwise mysterious thoughts, decisions and actions.

The destruction of the brazen head itself demonstrates how this dynamic works in the novel's climactic episode. The assembled forces of the King's men and the Lost Towers have gathered for a stand-off over the brazen head. Peter Peregrinus is drunk with the power of his belief in destiny fulfilled, and uses his lodestone to summon every person he has 'ever met or ever heard of in that district' (*BH* 323). If there are any lingering doubts about the phallic substitution of the lodestone, this description should dispel them:

> Deep into the top-curve of the bony arch between his belly and his thighs, and just above his generative organs, Petrus had dug the blunt, thick, staring-eyed cranium of the demonic

lodestone he persisted in calling 'Little Pretty', and while he dug it into himself, he had summoned into his presence every living person old or young, male or female, he had ever met or ever heard of in that district. (*BH* 323)

Here sexual desire and the will-to-power are indistinguishable. Peregrinus is able to compel others to do his bidding. His urges manifest themselves in the chaos around him. Unlike the very circumspectly presented violence in the rest of the narrative, the fight between Baron Maldung and Lady Lilt is as gruesome as Peregrinus's imagination: 'some devoted adherent of the mistress of the Castle smashed the master's skull with a heavy stone, and some furious armour-bearer of the murdered Maldung knelt on the lady and strangled her to death with his two hands, before his own head was severed from his crouching body and all three corpses were soaked in his blood' (*BH* 323).

This violent spectacle releases pent-up social energies, and the revolutionary Dod Pole seizes the opportunity to make common cause with his serf, whom he regards as his disciple:

> 'Yes, my friends, it is we who plough and sow and plant and reap and gather the harvest and bake the bread and butcher the meat! It is we, the shepherds and the hedge-planters, we, the cattle-tenders and the swine-herders, who own this sacred and holy and God-given earth of ours! … Handing down they are what they've stolen, from father to son, and son to grandson; and all the good earth and all the precious sea-shore of which they have robbed us curses them as wicked thieves! Come let us show them what we think of them! *To your tents, O Israel!*' (*BH* 324)

Immediately after Dod Pole's exhortation to his followers to storm Lost Towers, symbol of tyrannical baronial power, Lilith appears, and we read, as though in explanation, that 'it was as if their united will-power had called upon Lilith to appear' (*BH* 325). And as he watches Lilith Peregrinus is seized with lust and purpose, for it is he who has created this sacrificial violence and released this revolutionary energy. Before the moment can be fulfilled, however, Bonaventura appears and tries to defuse the tension. Peregrinus wavers between his lust for Lilith and his desire for self-preservation, and decides to flee the scene rather than attempt to exert his spiritual authority. This would be contested by Albertus Magnus, and Peregrinus is wary of the testing of his spiritual power. Spardo still follows Bonaventura, but in his flight he suppresses his violent nature only by grabbing the largest weapon he can find. Here is another manifestation of the lodestone's will-to-power. Drawn by Peregrinus's power, Spardo comes across Heber Sygerius who longs with all his will to be killed quickly and violently, with a dolorous blow. Spardo, in his blood-lust, deals such a blow without hesitation.

Meanwhile, after Dod Pole's rebellion, in which both bondmen and freemen tear off their clothes and follow him into the wilderness, Lilith and Petrus retreat into Lost Towers. Roger Bacon is watching the stars, and Albertus Magnus is preaching, and marrying couples quite indiscriminately. Bacon himself, in a curious aside, notes that Albertus had always despised the practice of older men marrying very young women. Is this directed at Petrus and Lilith? Or more generally at Albertus's apparent moral lapse in his carnivalesque enactments of the marriage service? By now we should be able to recognize the character-system when Roger Bacon is described as having taken Aristotle for granted with one side of his nature and the New Testament with the other, though without reconciling them; by contrast, Albertus Magnus has been able to bring the Classical and the Christian 'into logical opposition to each other and into logical relation with each other' (*BH* 335).

For his part, Magnus uses his scheme of logical oppositions to work out what he thinks about sex, 'the maddest force there is'

(*BH* 336). He desires to consecrate this force and thinks that the 'ceremonious consecration of the joining together of sex-mates has been the instinctive retort of all animal life to the insanity of sex from the beginning of the world' (*BH* 336). These thoughts are attributed to his conscience or 'guardian angel', though it is made clear that the marriage ceremony is the only way Albertus can come to terms with what he sees as the general shedding of inhibitions all around him. When he marries Tilton and Una, Lady Val is so incensed by the lack of decorum and her lingering resentment against Roger Bacon (who had not given her a magnetic charm she had requested, for assistance and protection in her affairs) that she attacks the brazen head — the symbolic centre and the focal point of her hatred — and damages it. When its creator sees this act of violence, he responds very calmly, and considers what it might mean that life is self-willing and self-willed. Acknowledging that the brazen head is now only 'one-fiftieth' alive, Roger Bacon remains adamant that it is still capable of speech under certain unusual circumstances.

These circumstances occur when Petrus and Lilith come out of the castle. Lilith holds the lodestone now, and with it she raises Lost Towers into the heavens. Moments before, Petrus had declared himself the antichrist; now, seizing the lodestone — as it were, the agent of the phallus — Lilith thrusts Petrus and herself into the heavens, whence they crash down in a fiery ball and smash the brazen head. The head had been speaking and was just about to complete its three-part utterance on the nature of time. Lost Towers itself has been one of the four points of topographical balance in the narrative, and its destruction signals the ensuing destruction of the antithetical pole of Petrus Peregrinus, and thus also of his antithesis, Roger Bacon.

There is no strong or obvious sense in which Roger Bacon can be seen as the hero of this romance. He is merely one of its generative poles, one in a series of character-spaces set in opposition and contradiction to each other, whose interplay permits the configuring of otherwise-random clusters of situations. Two features seem to determine this interplay. One is a consistent tendency towards the erotic — if not the pornographic — in the novel. Lilith in particular seems like a character out of the pornographic novels that Powys had once read so avidly, and the overt systematization of *The Brazen Head* might recall the similar abstractions of character seen in de Sade. The other structural feature is what might be called the 'unknown centre'; Powys takes the year 1272, virtually undocumented in the lives of his principal characters, and invents for it, as he invests in it, an alternate or 'animated' history which transforms it into the focal point of universal history. As already quoted, Powys claimed that he chose this date for no better reason that that it was precisely six hundred years before his own birth. It is this intense yet schematic mixture of the personal and the cosmic that makes this work perhaps the clearest example of Powys's novelistic method. *The Brazen Head* should not be regarded as a late novel of uncertain type and purpose, but as the very quintessence of his literary craft.

WORKS CITED

Brebner, John A., *The Demon Within: A Study of John Cowper Powys's Novels*. (New York: Harper, Row, 1973).

Cavaliero, Glen, *John Cowper Powys: Novelist*. (Oxford: Clarendon Press, 1973).

Christensen, Peter G., 'Frustrated Narration in *The Brazen Head*', *Powys Journal* XII (2002), 83-101.

——, 'Wessex, 1272: History in John Cowper Powys's *The Brazen Head*', *Powys Review* 21 (1987-1988), 28-35.

Connor, John T., *Mid-Century Romance: Modernist Afterlives of the Historical Novel*. Ph.D. dissertation, University of Pennsylvania, 2010. Available at: http://repository.upenn.edu/dissertations/AAI3447504

Goodwin, Jonathan, 'Nationalism and Re-enchantment in John Cowper Powys's *A Glastonbury Romance*', *Powys Journal* XVII (2007), 115-32.

Jameson, Fredric, *The Political Unconscious*. Ithaca (NY: Cornell University Press, 1981).

NOTES

1. Fredric Jameson uses the phrase 'character system' in *The Political Unconscious*, though he does not define it as thoroughly as Woloch (244).
2. I am referring throughout here to conceptual anachronism, not the material or technological form of anachronism which puts Shakespearean clocks in Caesar's Rome. By 'conceptual anachronism' I mean thought-systems and historical understandings not characteristic or even possible in the age depicted. A reading of Powys's work in terms of modernist revisions of the historical novel is to be found in Richard Maxwell, 'Two Canons' and *The Historical Novel in Europe*, and in John T. Connor, *Mid-Century Romance: Modernist Afterlives of the Historical Novel*.
3. Krissdóttir quotes from Powys's Diary of June 14, 1955.
4. Bonaventura appears set to function as the antithesis of Roger Bacon until we are introduced, rather belatedly, to Peter Peregrinus. It may then be the comparatively marginal Albertus Magnus who serves as the antithesis of Bonaventura.
5. Some details are taken directly from Westacott's *Roger Bacon in Life and Legend*: the name of Raymond de Laon is that of Bacon's trusted intermediary Rémond de Laon (22).
6. John A. Brebner stresses that Powys describes the brazen head as a magical not a scientific invention, its creation an 'act of worship' (212).
7. As is demonstrated thoroughly by Peter Christensen's 'Wessex, 1272: History in John Cowper Powys's *The Brazen Head*.
8. The meaning of the word *parthenos* has long divided interpreters of the New Testament, and there is an analogous ambiguity in Ghosta's sexual maturity; Roger Bacon thinks of her as a maiden though others clearly have a different view.
9. In a letter to Nicholas Ross, dated February 19, 1955, Powys writes: 'You asked me what I was writing now. Well, a Medieval Romance beginning and ending in the year 1272 just exactly 600 years before the birth of that appalling humbug and accursed SHAM. ... Yes, my romance begins and ends in the year of the Devil 1272. Just 600 years before at six A.M. in Shirley, Derbyshire, Charles Francis Powys and Mary Cowper Powys had their first-born child' (*Letters to Ross*, 127).

ARJEN MULDER

Into the World and Back Again: Reading Llewelyn Powys for the 21st Century *

The statement I originally wanted to make and the question I wanted to address is this: 'Llewelyn Powys started as a cosmopolitan writer and ended as a local writer, the opposite direction of the one every author has to take nowadays to become a success, both artistically and commercially. What did Llewelyn lose and what did he gain in this journey? And what are we losing and gaining if we follow the opposite direction?'[1] When I wrote this summary the example I had in mind of a contemporary author who started locally and ended as a cosmopolitan, or what I would prefer to call a global writer, is J.M. Coetzee.

Coetzee began writing novels about local South African problematics, but today his novels are about people operating on a global scale, involved with universally human, existential themes. First: *In the Heart of the Country* (1977) and *Life and Times of Michael K* (1983) are both about the mental and interhuman devastations of apartheid. Recently he has published *Elizabeth Costello* (2003) and *Diary of a Bad Year* (2007); the first is about the life and death, the lectures and conversations of a famous author who's travelling the entire globe, while the second takes place entirely in Australia, with connections to Germany and the Philippines.

The question that I posed remains interesting, but rereading Llewelyn and rethinking the idea, I understand that to answer it properly would need a thorough analysis of Llewelyn's style, and how it develops from the early autobiographical essays of the

* *A version of this essay was read at the Powys Society Conference, Street, August 2012.*

1920s, *Black Laughter, Skin for Skin* and *The Verdict of Bridlegoose*, into the mature style of his essays from the 1930s: *Earth Memories*, *Dorset Essays* and *Somerset Essays*. Such an analysis would require a thorough knowledge of the English language of the last, say, 500 years, and a real understanding of how the English language was transformed in the first half of the 20th century.

Yet I'm not able to recognize a word or expression as typically American or typically English, or typical for Dorset or typical for African English. So my original research question is more a hint for somebody else, more linguistically attuned, to pursue. But what I can do is look at Llewelyn and his literary output as a willing reader from outside the English-speaking world.

The journey that Llewelyn made, and the way his writing developed, makes a complex story; one way to enter it is through this question of the global and the local, which is partly a matter of the audience an author wishes to address. It is shocking that there is no recent biography of Llewelyn, nor a bestselling fictional version of his life. There's still just the one hagiography of Malcolm Elwin from 1946, hardly readable any more; and there's the essay *Llewelyn Powys* by Kenneth Hopkins, a true believer, from 1979. Richard Perceval Graves gives important details in *The Brothers Powys* (1983) and a lot of well-chosen quotes, but he doesn't try to interpret the goings-about and the writings and sayings of his main protagonists. Peter Foss's *Study of Llewelyn Powys: His Literary Achievement and Personal Philosophy* (1991), may supply some of these wants, but there's no copy of the book in Holland and I regret that I've not been able to consult it.[2]

I find Llewelyn's life as interesting as that of John Cowper Powys, about whom Morine Krissdóttir gave us a great sexual magical interpretation in *Descents of Memory* (2007). Why not try this with Llewelyn as well? Llewelyn's life is such a rich and strange story, both in situations and feelings: his position within the family as one of the younger sons, the extended travels he made, his meetings with important and well-known artists and writers, his position among the modernist avantgarde in New York. ... And then his love life, a girl in every city, the Golden Boy who glows in the dark, even when dying. His sexual triangle with an editor and a poetess, both in New York and in Dorset. And his heroic fight against tuberculosis. Here I want to explore some of this material, to introduce some themes that I would love to read about in a biography, or in a bestselling novel, neither of which I will ever write.

Llewelyn started as a writer with three autobiographical books about his consumption and how that both closed and opened the experience of life on earth for him. *Skin for Skin* is what I would call a global book. You don't have to know the political and social context of the story, because it's entirely him that's talking. It's this one voice, and how he modulates it, this one personality, this source of stylistic imagination, that one wants to listen to. One falls in love with Llewelyn's tone. That's an important observation: Llewelyn is the kind of writer who wants you, reader, to love him. The other option is of course to hate him, but I'm one of his lovers.

In *Skin for Skin* the tone of the first part in Clavadel, the sanatorium where he recovers from his tuberculosis near Davos in Switzerland, is entirely modern, fresh. The middle part in Dorset is a bit sluggish, the flow is slower and more intricate; it's what I would call local writing. The third part, back in the Swiss mountains, is global again. Llewelyn must have realized this himself, because a lot of what he tries to do and often achieves in his later essays is writing on local matters in a global, universally appealing tone. That is: no sluggishness but fresh in every single word; it's that freshness that we fall in love with, and that keeps us devoted.

When living in New York in the early roaring twenties Llewelyn writes and publishes *Black Laughter*, the second autobiographical book, with short-story-like essays about what he experienced in the five years he lived in East Africa as a colonial English farm manager. It's tough reading, because Llewelyn doesn't avoid the nasty bits. He's not so much honest as focused on his mental reactions to what the environment has to offer. What do I feel? That's the main question. What is my social and natural environment doing to me? The book is still hard to digest, even for Powysians. Of those I have met, one considers Llewelyn to be a racist. This he is not.

In a wonderful chapter, 'A Gentleman's Rebuke', Llewelyn tells about some of his first deeds after he was obliged to take over the runnning of a farm from his brother Will. The farm was on the edge of the jungle and the savannah and Llewlyn confesses that he caused an ecological catastrophe when setting fire to some grass. 'For nearly a week afterwards, as I lay on the veranda at night, I could follow the progress of that bush-fire.'[3] He goes on to describe his meeting with Somalian traders. 'When they saw me they would leave their mules and camels and with the utmost courtesy come over to talk to me in Swahili, telling me where they were going and about the cattle they had with them.'[4] The emphasis is of course on utmost courtesy.

One night one of the Somalis comes to the farm and asks if Llewelyn would allow him to sleep on the flax in the great barn. Later that evening the guest returns to the house and asks for an extra blanket. 'And because I had already acquired the provincial attitude of a white man in a black man's country, I felt disinclined to loan him any of my brother's blankets, but instead went and fetched a thick rug which was used for covering the kicking mule when the nights were chilly.'[5] Why is Llewelyn telling us this? Because he is a racist? No, because he wants to instruct us on what colonialism does to one's soul: it makes the Englishman provincial. The Somalis are not: they are cosmopolitans.

It's a matter of courtesy. Llewelyn continues: 'You know how the occasions in one's life when one has behaved especially crudely have a way of recurring to one's mind for years and years afterwards.'[6] Who is Llewelyn talking to, who is this 'You'? His fellow white men? No, the kind of readers Llewelyn wants to talk to. It is all about feeling, sensations, mental reactions, choices being made. Why doesn't Llewelyn invite the Somali into his house? And then the African feels cold and turns out to be a human just like him; but no, again Llewelyn doesn't invite him in by the fire, and instead gives him a thick and stinking rug for mules. Where did this utter lack of courtesy come from?

> I offered him the wrap; he looked at it, he saw the gray hairs on it and he returned it to me in silence, but with an expression on his proud finely bred features of such infinite contempt that I felt my ignoble action had in some way put me completely outside the pale of some unwritten standard of behaviour, taken for granted amongst gentlemen in the common-wealth of the human race.[7]

The most haunting scene in *Black Laughter* is another one that's open for dispute. In the chapter 'A Stockman's Hegira' he and his brother make a tour on horseback around the countryside. They steer their horses down to a river, the Milowa. 'We were within a few yards of it when, looking into a kind of ditch-like place, we saw the body of a native lying head downwards, with stiff beaded legs protuding grotesquely against the side of the bank. We passed on. I was in two minds to go back and discover what had killed the man in this out of the way place, but then remembered I was in Africa. After all it was none of my business. A dead nigger more or less, what did it matter?'[8]

I 'then remembered I was in Africa'. In a later chapter, 'On the Banks of the Guaso Nyiro', he meets a boy who tells him what killed the body they had left rotting on the banks of the Milowa. It turns out to be that of a Kikuyu boy who with his friend had tried to steal a bag of rice from Somali traders. When at midnight they crept into the camp, the boy was suddenly caught by the ankle. His friend escaped into the bush near the river bank. 'Meanwhile, the Somali, without a moment's thought, had unsheathed his ornamented knife and slit open the thief's navel as though he had been a jumping hare. He then put some more logs on to the fire and once more curled up to sleep.'[9] So much for Somali courtesy.

'The narrator concluded his story by simply remarking, "There is no fooling with Somalis." He then went on eating his pottage as though it was all past history.'[10] Africans, whether aristocrats or farmers, are utterly nihilistic when it comes to dead people: past history. Llewelyn rounds up: '"Certainly," I thought, as I entered the tent, "this is a land for the living. People have short memories in Africa for dead men."'[11] That is a very meaningful statement in the light of Llewelyn's later essays, and of the development of his style. In Africa Llewelyn learns what it means to have no long memory for the dead. But he has. He's from old stock, he's part of a long line, not from Anglo-Saxons, which he usually despises, but from … Indeed, from what, exactly?

Llewelyn was trapped in Africa for five years, due to the First World War, but finally returned to England, to Weymouth with its sands where his father was living. He writes local essays and tries to get them published, but to no avail. John Cowper comes to his rescue and takes him to the United States. Llewelyn had been there before his African exile, but had failed as a lecturer: this is an interesting detail when it comes to explaining Llewelyn's later tendency to go preaching. But this second time it's different. Llewelyn turns out to be a huge success in the literary circles to which John Cowper introduces him.

In my ideal biography this would be an extremely heavy chapter to write. What was JCP trying to achieve for and with Llewelyn when he transplanted him to New York? When it comes to John Cowper's motives one can't be paranoid enough. Beware of the sorcerer. What kind of creative energy was he trying to release in Llewelyn? Whatever it was, it worked: through John Cowper's intervention Llewelyn finally became a published author, a real writer.

The American adventures are the topic of the third autobiographical book, *The Verdict of Bridlegoose*, written after he had returned to Dorset. The original title was brilliant, *The American Jungle*, multi-layered symbol of exactly what Llewelyn was looking for in the United States. But John Cowper — perhaps seeking to avoid confuson with Upton Sinclair's novel *The Jungle* (1906) — had it replaced with a silly reference to Rabelais that nobody understands or cares about. This may be interpreted as a case of heavy sabotage by JCP against his younger brother. I imagine John Cowper explaining to Llewelyn that his point of view on America was that of a crazy European traveller, a mad old judge. This needed to be stressed in order to avoid trouble with the critics or even the police. Maybe the book was a bit too honest, both about its author and the people he's describing. If only Llewelyn had straigtened his back and stuck to *The American Jungle* his career might have followed an entirely different trajectory. The book could have been a hit, a new way of looking at life in New York, like some Truman Capote or Tom Wolfe from the 1920s.

Llewelyn stylizes himself like the tramp poet. He prefers to sleep on rooftops. He lives in dark and smelly rooms. He worries that someone might want to steal his old oil coat. He does his writing under the open sky on a shaky kitchen table in a back garden, and he only stops working when children come to play with him. He's like the troubadours Ezra Pound rediscovered in the Provence, but Llewelyn doesn't sing love songs; he's writing essays. There is a level of self-awareness in Llewelyn's writing that you will not often find in poetry. He knows what he's doing, and he's entirely authentic. In our own time a version of the tramp style that Llewelyn used would have been Amy Winehouse. Among Llewelyn's contemporaries was George Orwell, whose *Down and Out in Paris and London* (1933) might be seen as a contrast to 'Up and In in New York and San Francisco'.

Llewelyn the tramp is adored in higher places as yet another English eccentric. Americans recognize a natural when they meet one. Llewelyn is irresistible for young intellectuals of both sexes. He's invited to far more sophisticated parties than JCP ever made it to. He publishes his essays in *The Dial*; this is a very important historical fact. Llewelyn Powys steps right into the heart of the Modern Movement, and is recognized and acknowledged as one of the modernist authors, in line with Eliot, Joyce, Marianne Moore, trans-national, cosmopolitan, global. It will take a lot of research, careful reading and comparing to figure out what the modernists considered to be modernist in Llewelyn's autobiographical and literary essays.

I would suggest it was the tone of his writing. This tone is something to consider, because it is in the tone of the writing that one recognizes the local writer and the global one, or let us say, the old-fashioned and the modern author. What Llewelyn tried to do in the course of the two decades of his development as a writer was to fuse modern and ancient English vocabulary into one vivid and vital language, fit to express his happiness at being alive among the living while knowing about death.

Each of the three Powys brothers moves on a different plain of consciousness, a different plateau of awareness and sense of life. John Cowper's imagination is deeply mythical, chthonic; he reads Homer every day, the epic is his natural form. Theodore's is an allegorical literary strategy; every protagonist is part of an eternal story about the allure of death and the evil of what's alive. He reads the Bible and *A Pilgrim's Progress*.

In every study that I read Llewelyn is considered to be a realist. He is not. The theory of realism is a tough one, and I won't go into it now. Llewelyn's literary strategy is that of ballads and folktales. He moves on the mental level of the 'romance' as he calls it, the legendary plateau, not the mythical-symbolical or the allegorical one. Legends inform his imagination, his creative potential. The real isn't realistic but legendary in Llewelyn's poetic vision, both in his autobiographical books and his essays, but not in his ideologically-tainted philosophical works. I lack the vocabulary to go into details, but I know this much.

Legends are local stories. They are located, or locative. They are full of names both of persons and places. Fairy tales are long long ago in a far-away land, nowhere specific. Legends tell about singular happenings, one time only, unique events not to be forgotten in the memory of the people. Love, heroism, mental strength, the good life, death, all the great themes are to be found in legends, but they remain singular acts of particular people. There's a fixed set of characters that appear again and again in legends: the king, the beautiful girl, the old woman down the road, warriors and lovers, knights and bad guys. Legends do not sum up an all-encompassing myth, and they do not double into an allegorical narrative.

Llewelyn is the most personal of the three Powys brothers, not in an exhibitionist way like John Cowper, but as a friend you get to know. That's why you start to love him. There's no hidden agenda with Llewelyn. Maybe that's why he's considered to be a realist, but he is definitely not a reporter or a journalist. And he made his own life into the stuff that legends are made of. A Freudian interpretation of John Cowper's life and loves makes perfect sense, because he had consciously made his own life into the sort of myth that psychoanalysis deals with. With Llewelyn this doesn't seem to promise a new perspective. There may be some incestuous desire towards his sisters, but it would be no more than a psycho-analytical subplot. From the legendary perspective his behaviour makes much more sense.

A problem with Llewelyn's early autobiographical books seems to be that the old and the new do not really fuse in the final text. One finds classical or old-fashioned English terms in between modern expressions. It's hard for me to decide which is which, but I know Llewelyn is using an archaism whenever I have to grab my dictionary. We meet the same problem in the Little Blue Books that he published while in New York: *Honey and Gall*, again a ridiculous title for what is basically a short series of modern experiences, expressed in the form of essays on a wide range of topics, including satire and family jokes. An even worse title for another Little Blue Book was *Cupbearers of Wine and Hellebore*. Who started this ridiculous quoting of ancient English wisdom? It sounds like a high-brow Cambridge sort of humour to me. The Little Blue Books didn't sell until the publisher Haldeman-Julius changed the titles into *Studies in Mystic Materialism* and, even better, *A Book of Intellectual Rowdies*.

In both the autobiographical books and the essays the old and the new remain stylistic devices; they do not merge into one organic, timelessly modern stream of consciousness as they do in Dorothy M. Richardson's *Pilgrimage* or Proust's *In Search of Lost Time*. Llewelyn's essays are tatters of time, streamlets of consciousness, sometimes pleasantly flowing, as in the long essay *The Cradle of God*, and in the shorter essays compressed into moments of intense feeling. In Llewelyn's writings of the 1920s the old and new words are still in combat, not organically connected but colliding and short-circuiting. There is a sort of sparkling going on at the level of words in these books that infuses the level of the narrative with vivid and disturbing imagery.

In *The Verdict of Bridlegoose* Llewelyn mentions how he meets Scott Fitzgerald at a party, so one might suppose that he knew Fitzgerald's work. Scott Fitzgerald was a full-blown American modern writer, more purely modern than Hemingway or Pound or even Gertrude Stein. They were always nagging about other people, and since we can hardly remember who these petty authors or intellectuals or artists were, the books about them become old fashioned too. Scott Fitzgerald accepted all the oddities of the higher classes, just as Jane Austen accepted the funny moral codes of her time, and both showed in a timelessly modern, or should we say eternally contemporary way, the comedies and tragedies that follow from the play of classes and gender codes. Llewelyn might even have undertaken the merging and fusion of American and European culture that was a characteristic of some of the most ambitious projects of modernism, notably in Ezra Pound's *Cantos* and in Gertrude Stein.

Llewelyn's precision when describing emotional responses from the inside out is distinctly modern. He has the ability to make you feel and see what you're reading about. He wanted to live the old, he tried to upload the old into the new, and even when it sounded funny, as it often did, he wouldn't give up. And when it worked, it finally became an organic process of growth and sympathy. Llewelyn wrote one masterpiece of long essayistic writing, a perfect fusion of an ancient and a modern mind. But it is a contested book, *The Cradle of God* (1929), a recounting of the Bible in terms of Llewelyn's own visit to the Holy Land.

At this point in the story the bestselling novel would take off. The plot is getting more intricate if not complicated. Female passion enters the scene. Llewelyn meets Alyse Gregory, editor of *The Dial*. She is his umpteenth girl in New York, but this time something happens and he falls in love with her. Alyse Gregory was a strong woman who had been a suffragette, a fighter for women's rights, a rebel, and a very critical observer of any relationship between men and women. She was a professional, an editor at a magazine that created the avantgarde as much as it was created by it; she was in the place to be if you were a literary editor in America in the 1920s. And of all people Alyse Gregory also fell in love with Llewelyn and his ridiculously old-fashioned coat, and hat, and points of view.

In the early summer of 1922 Llewelyn moved into Alyse's apartment at 4 Patchin Place in Greenwich Village. He was writing African essays and *Skin for Skin*, and she was editing him. Alyse herself started to write and publish her own books as well: three modernist novels, based on her life with Llewelyn. But then his consumption played up again, he spat blood, he had to move out of the city, and settled in a small house near the Catskill Mountains. And Alyse joined him there to care for him, to be his lover, his nurse and his assistant, while travelling to New York every day to edit *The Dial* — not least, in October 1922, to publish in its pages *The Waste Land* by T.S. Eliot.

Alyse was Llewelyn's lifeline to modern literature, his connection with the contemporary writing of his age. The history of the relations between authors and their female editors has yet to be written but is fertile ground for research. After two happy years full of compromises for Alyse, Llewelyn decides it's easier to get married. For him it's just an administrative thing; it makes travelling less expensive. But for Alyse it feels like a betrayal of everything she fought for all her life. She knows she is losing part of her autonomy, her independence, and yet she submits.

'I WANT TO COME HOME.'[12] That's how Llewelyn explains his decision to go back to Dorset. He needs a more direct lifeline to the living soil, the place of his origin. He wants to live in a cottage on top of the highest cliff of Dorset, the White Nose, where day after day the storms and showers come banging in from over the Atlantic Ocean. Llewelyn is challenging his consumption by defying the elements, the torrents of rain and the gales, like some Cuchulain maybe, some crazy king of old legends and ballads. But for Alyse it means she has to quit her job at *The Dial*, and move to what would have seemed to her a most provincial place.

In *The Verdict of Bridlegoose* Llewelyn tells about his first meeting with Alyse Gregory at Patchin Place, gathered into one long, meandering sentence, moving from context to intimacy to fantasy and memory:

> These rooms suggested to my mind my rooms in the Old Court of Corpus, and were entirely different from anything I had seen elsewhere in New York, as, indeed, was the poise, the intellectual intensity, the freedom from preconceptions, as of a child uncontaminated by the world, of my grave, delicately ironic hostess, whose round, white arms seemed to me then, as I looked at them in the flickering light of the cannel-coal fire, as delectable as dairy junket, and whose fair hair, worn so as to conceal as far as possible the prominence of an over-high forehead, was of a fairer and more fine texture than ever was the hair of that lovely chatelaine who so long ago would sit beneath the glittering holly trees of Brittany, watching her madcap children playing in the coarse seaside grass.[13]

The minute he sees her Llewelyn associates Alyse Gregory with the coast of England. Traditional furniture, yet modern in outlook, 'as of a child uncontaminated by the world'. What's happening here? Either he is blind or she is pretending to be something that she isn't. Llewelyn seems to be projecting a desire onto Alyse that she is not willing or able to fulfil. She is not at all the sort of person to sit watching madcap children in the seaside grass. She's an independent woman in one of the power centres of modern culture; no fair lady from a folk song, but a city woman with a busy social life and a brilliant career.

But Alyse lets herself be transported by her fairy prince to the White Nose, of all places. And within a few months there's nothing left of her, the winds have blown out all her poise; her intellectual intensity, her freedom, her entire mental life and personality have gone. She arrived at October 22, 1925. After only eight months, on June 5, 1926, she wrote in her diary those words that give the title to the published selection from her diaries: 'A solitary walk down to the sea, the fresh wind, the waves breaking at my feet, washing over the shining rocks, the dazzling sun. How terrifying is human consciousness, no more substantial than the cry of a single gull.'[14]

'No', one wants to shout at Alyse: 'Consciousness doesn't last the two or three seconds that such a cry takes, yours has been busy for forty years already, you're an adult, a mature person, do please think, think.' But in the diary her thinking remains entirely insubstantial, unstable, mostly self-sabotage for at least the next three years, and basically until Llewelyn's death in 1939.

After two years on top of the cliffs Alyse is getting some of her wits back, and talks Llewelyn into visiting New York again. Her return to civilization turns out to be yet another fatal step for Alyse. Back in Patchin Place with John Cowper and his new love Phyllis Playter, Llewelyn meets the new neighbour, the 'little poetess' Gamel Woolsey. Alyse takes a weekend off to visit her parents, so as to let Llewelyn and Gamel have their pleasure. And they do. And when Alyse returns she sort of falls in love with Gamel too.

Gamel is indeed the lovely chatelaine beneath the glittering holly trees that Alyse never was. Alyse agrees that Gamel is the one that Llewelyn was looking for. So she takes on another role. This time, in order to save her marriage, she carries off Llewelyn, out of New York and back into the storms on the White Nose. Llewelyn doesn't want to leave, but Alyse soothes him with a promise: We'll make that pilgrimage to the Holy Land that you have been talking about for so long. And indeed they leave the Dorset downs, and travel via Athens and Turkey to Jerusalem. There they stop at the post office and find a letter from Gamel, telling them that she had had a miscarriage; she had lost Llewelyn's child after an accident with a cab, though it was a rather confused story.

The couple decide to travel around Palestine for a few more weeks; Llewelyn has to do his research for the books he has contracted. He lies down in the original grave of Joseph of Arimathea, the one in which Jesus was buried for three days. Consumption time again. They stop travelling and settle on Capri for the winter. And there, on that quiet island, in his bereavement over his dead child, Llewelyn writes *The Cradle of God*.

The book is especially interesting because it suggests that Llewelyn could have been a far more interesting and greater writer if he had stuck to the belief of his childhood. *The Cradle of God* proves that he was a born believer. He really feels his way into the Christian faith. As a professing atheist he is far less convincing and doesn't rise above the level of ideology. But when he allows himself to be religious, he rises to an empathetic and sympathetic level of understanding that is universally human, instead of repeating the outmoded rhetoric of atheism and anti-clergy hobby-horsing dating from the late 19th century.

The Cradle of God begins with Llewelyn setting out to understand the true significance of the Christian faith, the faith of his forebears, his father, his civilization. He sits on a bank by the side of a downland track, looks into the night sky, and proclaims: 'Mystery beyond mystery, space beyond space, and against them the belief of my heritage like a single candle flickering in the void, like a wooden match struck for a moment in a heathen temple.'[15]

That may sound like a critical statement, but there are no anti-religious feelings here. Llewelyn explores a living faith, the beliefs of his heritage, its gesture against the void, not the cry of a single gull, but a match of self-awareness struck in a heathen temple of unconscious fears and desires.

Llewelyn proposes a new way to study the Bible: 'Christian arguments are false arguments, Christian thoughts shallow thoughts; yet, even so, these prayerful madcaps have hold, perhaps, of some invisible clue denied to ruder natures. And it is with such an assumption in our minds that we must approach the legendary fables on which they lay such store. The yearnings of the human heart have created a religious poetry, pure and simple, and it would be unbecoming to mock at the expression of so much authentic feeling. Symbolism it is, allegory it is, but it is also the voice of deep-hidden longings, the child of tears.'[16] That's what a legend is: 'the voice of deep-hidden longings, the child of tears.' I find that a stunning definition.

Says Llewelyn: 'Conceived in this way it may be possible for us to regard these infantile and presumptuous displays without irritation.'[17] So again: who's this 'us'? Llewelyn is writing for an audience of non-believers, but indeed he has got them irritated, not so much with the Bible, but with his own study of it.

A case in point is the essay of Kenneth Hopkins on Llewelyn Powys. First Hopkins claims that the *Cradle of God* is a *tour-de-force*, in the negative sense: 'here are things not inherent in the writer's genius, not characteristic of those special skills and aptitudes which are his alone.'[18] The book 'could have been written by another, and might not have been the worse for that.' In short: the book does not fit into our expectations of Llewelyn.[19]

That's heavy if not harsh criticism, but then Hopkins makes a flip: 'To say this is not to dismiss or condemn *The Cradle of God*. In this book Llewelyn Powys reaches a maturity as a writer of English prose, a maturity which indeed is foreshadowed and almost attained in *Skin for Skin*, but not quite with the effortless authority displayed here.'[20] So *The Cradle of God* is Llewelyn's most mature book, yet Hopkins would have preferred that Llewelyn was not its author.

In a third and last evaluation of the book Hopkins makes an even stronger statement: 'But *The Cradle of God* is pretty generally free of stylistic weakness, and page after page can be read for the pleasure of the language.'[21] 'Here there are no "recurrent corpses", no "haugty heavens"; there is not a word that could be exchanged for another with profit. This is the voice of conviction, too much taken up with that conviction to have a thought to "style".'[22] I take that to be a compliment.

No overwrought style, a discipline of language where not a word can be replaced. That seems to me to be the highest praise possible for any book or author. And I fully agree, and I am very happy that Llewelyn wrote it, because it's just the kind of book that only he could ever write. Llewelyn was very nervous about it: was it not boring? But John Cowper gave it his seal of approval, and Llewelyn sent it from Capri to Jonathan Cape in London.

When *The Cradle of God* was published a year later, the couple were back in Dorset after their pilgrimage and their life had utterly changed. From New York John Cowper had written a letter asking Llewelyn to take back Gamel and let her come over to Dorset as well: she is so miserable after the loss of your child, she needs your company. So Gamel Woolsey moved into a cottage a little inland from the cliff-top holiday cottage that Llewelyn and Alyse were living in. It is understood that Gamel has come over for a second chance to bear Llewelyn's child.

Gamel Woolsey's legendary Gestalt is the fairy, the dancing butterfly-like pixie who seduces the fauns and satyrs she's playing with deep in the woods and the wilderness. She is living in a legendary universe just outside the one we spend our lives in, a *Middle Earth* that gave the title to her first collection of poems, and was of course later used by Tolkien for *Lord of the Rings*. When people met Gamel she somehow didn't seem to be entirely there, and yet she was more present than most other people. In Dorset for a few miraculous months in 1929 she and Llewelyn lived the life of Middle Earth, in the ditches and cottages and hayfields wherever they found the traces of the otherworld. Llewelyn was the only man in her life that was able to enter Middle Earth with her and live the real life of the imagination in actual woods and fields.

Never to be forgotten. In Clavadel, shortly before he died, Llewelyn wrote Gamel in his last letter to her about the children in the village, how he couldn't give them too much attention. 'They seem to lead me very near to our secret garden and often as I play with them I seem to be playing with you.'[23] For bystanders their Middle Earth afternoons and evenings must have been somewhat childish and sexually charged; for the lovers it was the best part of their lives.

He continues his letter: 'Often a token, a gesture, a word at the end of a letter, can evoke in a moment the eyebright, the thyme, the quivering sunshine of the banks of Maiden Castle, the silent magic of Dorset woods, and the easy valley where we used to walk. In those flint fields when your tall boots were muddy, how lovely it was for me to feel you near — your warm beautiful lovely body so near — as we walked looking and stooping over those austere plough lands where the sea winds go.'[24] And under this last letter he scribbles: 'Darling,

darling Gamel, my darling, I love you.' And dies only two weeks later.

Imagine a book with the unabridged letters of Llewelyn and Gamel. Now they have been separately published in *So Wild a Thing* and *The Letters of Gamel Woolsey to Llewelyn Powys 1930-1939*. In our book Llewelyn's letters would be on the upper part of the page. In the published letters of Llewelyn to Gamel long passages are skipped, especially where Llewelyn seems to regress into the mental state of a child, but I would love to read these fantasy bits because that's what Middle Earth is all about. Under Llewelyn's letters is a second horizontal range with Gamel's answers, chronologically ordered and placed so as to allow the reader to see the story unfold. Gamel's letters are wonderful, light of tone and yet intense, rather chaotic, jumping in time while being written, but always Gamel only.

There's a third horizontal band on the lower half of the page for the unabridged diary of Alyse Gregory, again chronologically linked to the letters above. In the legendary set-up around the cottage on the White Nose where Gamel is a fairy and Llewelyn a satyr, Alyse turns into both a white mother and a black witch. She is the Mother in the sense of the caring wife who creates the right conditions for Llewelyn's writing. Rearing a child is also a form of editing, so why not the other way round?

But in their cottage on the White Nose Alyse becomes mother in another sense too, doing the chores and the shopping, and available whenever Llewelyn wants to sleep with her. A quote from Alyse's diary: 'After tea he embraced me and I stood later looking out over the fields thinking that I have never been wholly free in my embraces with Llewelyn because he never reaches the core of my being.'[25] That's a most depressing description of sex in the afternoon. Addicted to a lover who never reached the core of her being because, I suppose, she never gave him the child he longed for. She failed to become a real mother.

Alyse's diary is like a thick stream of dark bile, of gall and hellebore, the venom of a woman utterly jealous yet allowing herself no such natural feelings. A poisonous text, spoiling all our joy about both Llewelyn and Gamel with a mud of petty feelings and repressed hate and resentment. Another way of looking at these eruptions of disgust and self-hate is to consider them as the emotional problems that the first generation of feminists had to go through, before they could get on with their lives. 'He has never really conquered me', Alyse keeps repeating in her diary.[26] 'Oh, miracle of miracles — I have felt quiver the breath of life — of my life, separate, without disgrace, without fear.'[27] That is: without Llewelyn. His legendary lifestyle has nearly extinguished her independent self, but there is still some kernel left, a secret well of loneliness in Llewelyn's company.

Gamel becomes pregnant again. Llewelyn is again utterly happy. The doctor tells Gamel that she won't survive the birth of her child due to her tuberculosis. She has an abortion, leaving her body bruised, and Llewelyn devastated with a new attack of his own consumption, spitting blood and nearly dying, and Alyse full of pity for both of them and full of hatred against her own failure to give him the child he needs. To escape the sad situation Gamel agrees to marry Gerald Brenan, who happens to come along, and thus moves out of Llewelyn's circle of influence.

After the first severe attacks of tuberculosis Llewelyn stayed mostly in his open shelter on the downs. There he started to write what was eventually to become *Love and Death*, intended to be his final masterpiece. When Gamel married Brenan and moved to Spain, he stopped working on the text, feeling utterly frustrated, sad and old. It wasn't until three years later, in 1936, while staying for the third and last time in Clavadel, that he continued writing the book, finishing it in 1939.

Alyse helped him with his writing, as she calls the process of editing in her diary. Along the way he produced essays for periodicals, hundreds of them: the list in Peter Foss's *Bibliography* is staggering. But I want to concentrate briefly on this 'imaginary autobiography' *Love and Death*, searching for an answer to my question of local versus global writing.

The most surprising sentence in both the English and the American editions of *Love and Death* is to be found in Alyse Gregory's Introduction, where she says of the book: 'It is old-fashioned and at the same time extremely modern.'[28] An interesting statement indeed. What did Alyse consider to be modern in *Love and Death*? It is a book full of sentences in which 'the luxuriance of the imagery sometimes overbalances the main thought of the sentence'[29] — and that's nicely put by Alyse.

This is definitely local writing. It tells the story of the first love affair of Llewelyn when he was 23 years old, with a girl called Dittany Stone, whom both Alyse and Gamel knew to be a persona of Gamel in the time of their love affair. But the peculiar thing is that the book is written in what one might call a tone of elegiac realism. There is no sign of Middle Earth to be found in the story. It's legendary, indeed, but a different legend than the one they had lived in during their miracle year on the Dorset downs after her miscarriage.

The first sixty pages are superb. Llewelyn describes his attack of consumption, yet another confrontation with death, and recovering in his shelter on the downs he remembers his first love. It is a memory, but with a vitality that is used as a counterforce or medicine against death's approach. After that, I suppose when Llewelyn continued his writing on Alyse's instigation, it loses some of its intensity and compactness, perhaps because he is explaining what he is trying to evoke instead of just evoking it.

So for example he writes: 'It was extraordinary how, when we were together, some imaginative affinity, some native physical susceptibility, made it possible for us to step clean out of time and enter freely into some new world of our own where romance was instant in the very grass leaves, in the very mud that received the pressure of her heels.'[30] That same observation he made in the first 60 pages, but there he evoked it beautifully as happening 'in the time that is always over the hedge, always beyond each gatepost, always on the other side of the next hill.'[31]

In chapter 23 Llewelyn rails against the clergy for no particular reason, but even before the book was published, Llewelyn wrote to H. Rivers Pollock: 'I believe the book would have been better if I had left out the polemical chapter'.[32] So why didn't he remove it? Where was editor Alyse when author Llewelyn needed her? The freshness returns in the evocation of the first night they make love, on a bed under an apple tree in the orchard, a wonderful, shining piece of writing, both exciting and heartbreaking.

In *A Woman at her Window*, her excellent booklet on Alyse Gregory, Jacqueline Peltier makes an amazing discovery in an unpublished part of Alyse's diary, without expanding on it. Alyse mentions her problems while editing *Love and Death* in having to 'relive those nightmarish times again and again.'[33] meaning the summer of love of 1929. Llewelyn is amazed by this *domestic* view of the book, but 'he said he would burn the mss. if it gave me any unhappiness, for he could take no pleasure in it if it caused me distress. But I reassured him and advised him to take out all the last chapters when he returns to earth to me, which overbalance it and give it something strained and bizarre. And we went over it together again and he took out much that was irrelevant; and I praised it *very* much, and he is happy now about it.'[34]

So editor Alyse deletes herself out of Llewelyn's imaginary autobiography. Where are these lost chapters now? Have they ever been reprinted? I'd love to read them, because I feel a suspicion that Alyse played a trick on Llewelyn, she took revenge. The *Love and Death* from the title in the current, shortened edition refer to Llewelyn's love and death. But if there was a second part of the book about Alyse, that would suggest that Gamel had the Love-part and Alyse represented Death. It's your imaginary autobiography, Alyse must have thought, not mine. I'll make it into your imaginary nightmare, not mine. This would also account for not taking out the irrelevant Chapter 23, maybe even encouraging Llewelyn to retain it. Am I paranoid? Yes, but this simply screams for further research, probably imaginary, perhaps in a novel.

The autograph manuscript of *Love and Death* in three quarto notebooks (Add. MS 7664/1-3) is in the Manuscripts Department of Cambridge University Library. Earlier versions are to be found, Peter Foss tells me, in the Humanities Research Center in the University of Texas in Austin. Studying them might give a clue as to why Alyse Gregory calls the book not just old-fashioned but at the same time extremely modern. Is this the kind of writing in which the old has finally fused with the new? Llewelyn had been striving towards this all his life. Is this the merging of the local with the global? Are we simply not yet mature enough to see the modern and old now timelessly fused in it? It's quite an effort to read *Love and Death*, but it gives a very good aftertaste. Why did John Cowper approve? Was this what he had been aiming for with Llewelyn?

John Cowper suggests a solution to the problem of the unbalancedness in *Love and Death*, and I will end with this. Shortly after Llewelyn's death he makes in his diary a shocking note, with 'a hint of his usual antagonism toward Alyse' as Jacqueline Peltier calls it,[35] but I would say: with the X-ray vision of the clair-voyant, the super psychologist who's always studying people's emotional strategies and peculiarities, the global cosmopolitan sympathetic view of the people he loves that is way beyond any antagonism or neurosis, the most moving example of brotherly love that I know of. I'll quote it from *Petrushka and the Dancer*:

> My Lulu is the humorous poetical *earthy stylist* & original personality; *hers* is what *her* life-illusion loved best (& Lulu *was influenced* by it) pontifical, grave, ungullible, *distinguished* ... But this Lulu — *my* Lulu — is not less of a personality or less of a *true* personality — but *much more!* for as with all the great humorists loved by Lulu — like Chaucer for instance — the power to see yourself ... as no more 'right' or 'grand' or 'truthful' or 'distinguished' *than those others* — but *just yourself*, with all your weaknesses — was one of Lulu's most bewitching endearing & in the deepest sense of all, *sagacious* peculiarities. And this peculiarity, Alyse naturally and inevitably just because she *was* Lulu's feminine companion *set herself to destroy!*[36]

I think John Cowper is right, and it may be a clue as to why Llewelyn never succeeded in becoming the real global author — an author, also, of global fame and stature — that he might have been, and that some of us surely believe he ought to have been.

WORKS CITED

Gregory, Alyse, *The Cry of a Gull, Journals 1923-48*, ed. Michael Adam (Brushford, Dulverton, Somerset: The Ark Press, 1973).
Hopkins, Kenneth, *Llewelyn Powys* (London: Enitharmon Press, 1979).
Peltier, Jacqueline, *Alyse Gregory: A Woman at her Window* (London: Cecil Woolf, 1999).
Powys, John Cowper, *Petrushka and the Dancer: The Diaries of John Cowper Powys 1929-1939*, ed. Morine Krissdóttir (Manchester: Carcanet Press, 1995).
Powys, Llewelyn, *Black Laughter* (London: Grant Richards, 1925).
——, *The Verdict of Bridlegoose* (London: Jonathan Cape, 1927).
——, *Love and Death: An Imaginary Autobiography* (London: John Lane, The Bodley Head, 1939).
——, *The Letters of Llewelyn Powys* (London: John Lane The Bodley Head, 1943).
——, *The Cradle of God* (London: Watts, 1949).
——, *So Wild a Thing: Letters to Gamel Woolsey*, ed. Malcolm Elwin (Brushford, Dulverton, Somerset: The Ark Press 1973).

NOTES

[1] My own summary in advance of the conference talk, in *The Powys Society Newsletter* No. 75, March 2012, 7.
[2] I would like to propose that Foss's book should be made available digitally, or by Print on Demand, via the Powys Society Website.
[3] *Black Laughter*, 68.
[4] *Black Laughter*, 69.
[5] *Black Laughter*, 70.
[6] *Black Laughter*, 70.
[7] *Black Laughter*, 70.
[8] *Black Laughter*, 209.
[9] *Black Laughter*, 220.
[10] *Black Laughter*, 220.
[11] *Black Laughter*, 220-1.
[12] *Letters of Llewelyn Powys*, 121.
[13] *Verdict of Bridlegoose*, 73-4.
[14] *The Cry of a Gull*, 20-2.
[15] *The Cradle of God*, 1.
[16] *The Cradle of God*, 138.
[17] *The Cradle of God*, 138.
[18] Hopkins, *Llewelyn Powys*, 41.
[19] Hopkins, *Llewelyn Powys*, 41.
[20] Hopkins, *Llewelyn Powys*, 41.
[21] Hopkins, *Llewelyn Powys*, 43-4.
[22] Hopkins, *Llewelyn Powys*, 43-4.
[23] *So Wild a Thing*, 94.
[24] *So Wild a Thing*, 94.
[25] *So Wild a Thing*, 95.
[26] *The Cry of a Gull*, 65.
[27] *The Cry of a Gull*, 63.
[28] *Love and Death*, xiv.
[29] *Love and Death*, xi.
[30] *Love and Death*, 210.
[31] *Love and Death*, 58.
[32] *Letters of Llewelyn Powys*, 254.
[33] Peltier, *Alyse Gregory*, 32.
[34] Peltier, *Alyse Gregory*, 32.
[35] Peltier, *Alyse Gregory*, 6.
[36] John Cowper Powys, *Petrushka and the Dancer*, 334.

ALYSE GREGORY

The Limitations of the English Mind *

A recent article by Mr. Richard Church in which he criticises the attitude of his countrymen towards poetry rouses us to wonder if the English mind, outside literary circles, is one that lends itself to any indulgence towards ideas in whatever form they may show themselves. We have but to think of a Frenchman, an American, a Spaniard to realise the difference. A Frenchman may be provincial, but he is at ease at once in all discussions touching on the fundamental problems of human existence — on religion, on art, on sex. He may have a strong personal bias, but he has a mind open to argument, witty in rebuttal, and with no barriers against strangeness. He may feel that Paris is the centre of the universe and that too much beer and tea drinking is conducive to sallow complexions and sluggish cerebration, but in spite of his prejudice and arrogance his sensibility is hospitable to all intellectual discussions, his aplomb is an essentially civilised aplomb based on reason, courtesy, and usage.

As for the American, he may balance ideas as a juggler balances balls; he may be inept, cynical, lacking in *finesse*, brutal even, but his mind is always open to discussions. He approaches them innocently, adventurously, and with a kind of spontaneous candour that is racy and fearless but at the same time engagingly modest.

But how is any thought that is unorthodox, or even that dips one inch below the level of the complacent commonplace greeted by average Englishmen? Regard their faces as they move toward their business offices, their club rooms, their theatres — what a phlegmatic, barbarous acceptance of the surface values of life,

* First published in the *Adelphi*, November 1939.

what a frozen decorum, as if they had each one sipped from the ice-cold fountain that caused the death of Tiresias. If you happen to belong to a more analytical and restive nation, one where class distinctions are less rigid and mental eagerness more headlong, you will soon be brought to order should you be so unwise as to give rein to your interrogatory intelligence. It does not matter into what class or circle you enter. If you are so fortunate as to be invited to visit in a country house where the extraordinary beauty of the garden and the spacious calm of the old Elizabethan manor stir your admiration, you will soon learn to govern your feelings when the butler opens the door and you see graven upon his sober and serene countenance the long history of unquestioning servility, his timorous, unswerving, pompous, and abject loyalty to a fixed social order. And when the neat maid brings you your early morning tea her tensely sealed lips, her circumspect manner, her silent obsequious movements are another reminder that there are barriers that must not be challenged. 'Are we not both women, subject to sorrow, with a heart that was set beating by the same mysterious cause, and with senses that reach out to life in the same identical manner?' you feel like whispering to her. How easy it would be to stir an impulsive response from any French, Italian or American servant! The door closes, everything has been done for your comfort, but your spirit is not at rest.

Then you go down to your host. A handsome, genial, extremely well-bred man, a conscientious landlord, a member of many civic boards and benevolent organisations, well informed on all matters touching husbandry and politics, with a clear brain, a retentive memory and a kind heart, he is as closed to any entrance of ideas which challenge the traditions in which he has been brought up as the stout walls of his house to the entrance of all weathers. On everything that threatens to pierce one inch below the well ordered routine of his agreeable, bustling days he directs merely a bland, blank stare.

THE LIMITATIONS OF THE ENGLISH MIND

But let us return our attention to the very centre of culture itself, to the average don in the great English universities. Is it here that we shall find the hot furnace of fearless thought sending out its streams of light to illumine the bewildered brains of earnest students? Here is learning enough to cram the heads of all the youth in the world — and yet how dry, how meaningless, how sterile all instruction can be that is forced through a narrow channel of fixed principles, an instruction that does not present as the one cardinal necessity of all true education an open mind exposed with unprejudiced individual receptivity to every fact that is offered to it. There is, it would seem, hardly any group in the British Isles where the yawning gap between the assiduously employed intellect and the honest summing up of wayward human experience is more apparent than in these formidable and weighty assemblies of learned gentlemen in their impressive caps and gowns.

And if we now determine to concentrate on the scientists it is not much better, for these pale, 'sincere' scrutinisers of the elusive properties of solid matter, these distributors of the verity of the 'isolated fact' are as refractory before the free and disinterested play of ideas as anyone else. We have but to dwell on the general attitude of scientists to the use of animals for laboratory purposes, a subject in their opinion outside debate and only challenged by sentimentalists, to court a civil disapproval. What scientist would be seriously troubled by the following statement which I read recently in an article on insomnia in a monthly journal? 'Healthy dogs died after 14 days of enforced wakefulness, and rabbits after 21 days'. Where do we find one of them honest enough to say quite clearly 'Man has power over the animals of creation and he uses this power in a cruel and inhuman way to achieve his own ends?' That would be a simple and true statement, but one with disturbing implications, implications unpleasant to the ears of these unimaginative and conscientious men not disposed to investigate with cold reason a traffic so questionable.

Last of all, let us go to that inner circle of instructed literati — that inner circle of an inner circle — who by their university education, sophisticated manners, and apparent knowledge of the world would lead us to believe that their minds moved as freely and flexibly among ideas as negroes among sugar cane. What a surprise we receive when we discover that with these suave, weary, clever initiates of culture, though indeed they are shock-proof enough, ideas are received in an even more discouraging manner! They are not disliked for being dangerous or subversive, but merely as revealing in the mention a droll betrayal of naivety, or even of bad form. And truly this attitude of superciliously raised eyebrows before questions about unsettled and eternal matters, questions which would be received and answered with simple seriousness by any cultured Frenchman, Russian, or German is the most discouraging attitude of all. One's words strike a smooth surface and melt like snow on asphalt. The practised, ironical, imporous, hollow amiability of these people is maintained, apparently, not on a foundation of 'suffering and ardour' which we feel so often underlies the brilliance of French youth, but more on an equivocal foundation of suspicion, indifference, and an uneasy and self-protective self-consciousness.

It is puzzling to find a reason why so notable and honourable a people as the English, a people with so rich a literature and so great a love of liberty should be so lacking when it comes to the free play of the mind. Is the root of the matter perhaps to be discovered in the fact that the English people groan under the bondage of the two fixations — an ingrained sense of moral responsibility and fear of corrupting society, and an absurd class consciousness? There is no greater steriliser to the free play of the intellect than fear. The minute some monitor of caution steps in between us and our thinking processes the search for truth is already lost. The average Englishman thinks what he thinks he should think, and says what he supposes he thinks; and the kernel of his true insight lies as lost to him as a locked chest at the bottom of the sea he rules. The most informed mind will become automatically dull when it is dominated by a sense of deference and insecurity. Perhaps if the English mind were less honest and less well-disposed it would be more reliable. The very fact that an Englishman takes life with so sober a compulsion makes his thinking both ponderous and vague. He does not wish to be a hypocrite, so he leaves unpalatable thoughts well out of reach. What you don't touch can't bite you. A Frenchman is philosophic enough to be irresponsible, he will display his own inconsistencies with a clarity, precision, and vivacity that render them at once amusing and interesting. But even more disastrous to illuminating lawless thought is the awe that every Englishman feels towards the class scarce a thumb's width above him in station. There are only two groups of people who are in the least exempted from this obsessing preoccupation, the very poor whose search for bread keeps their attention close to the marrow of life, and who, since they can fall no lower in the social scale, view the panorama of existence with the unimplicated careless eyes of artists, and the aristocracy, who, being unable to rise any higher, feel the uncircumscribed freedom of that upper air of privilege, where, in their silks and satins, and blest with the emancipation of outlaws, they can pursue their *espiègleries* indifferent to public opinion. Snobbishness exists, of course, everywhere in the world, but not quite as marvellously as it does in England. It is only necessary to recall the words that have been invented to express a sense of shadowy social differences — 'outsider', 'cad', 'bounder', and the objectionable imported Anglo-Indian word, 'pukka' — all words whose nice discriminations are exactly understood by every

British subject. True culture pays no homage to such estimates. It is daring, sensitive, malleable, mutinous, resourceful, and blood-quick, and it does not base its judgments on anything but the garnered wisdom of its own critical and unbiassed evaluations.

Newspaper cutting marked on back: 'Alyse Dial Days'

Mary Butts (Re)viewing Llewelyn Powys's Dorset

Edited with an introduction by Joel Hawkes

Mary Butts (1890-1937) is a lesser-known modernist novelist, poet and writer of short stories. Her friends and acquaintances included Evelyn and Alex Waugh, Jean Cocteau, E.M. Forster, Ezra Pound, Charles Williams and Douglas Goldring. In the 1920s, she was part of the British and American expatriate community living in France, moving between Paris and the French Riviera. Her storytelling, however, is repeatedly and obsessively located in England; she remained enamoured of the Dorset of her childhood that held the enchanted memories of her family's 21-acre estate of Salterns in Parkstone, overlooking Poole Harbour. The decline and eventual sale of this childhood sanctuary, coupled with the social changes — especially suburbanization — that she witnessed ravaging the countryside, both haunt and structure her writing. Butts's Dorset is a mythical space, under threat, a place of ritual, magic and natural wonder that must be defended against the encroachings of modernity.

Butts's work has much in common with the writings of the brothers Powys; it shares a topography with T.F. Powys's fiction and with Llewelyn's essays, though it is more especially the 'Wessex' writings of John Cowper which resemble Butts's creations; drawing on the mythologies of the land, both seek to renew the landscape's primal potencies through acts of storytelling. We might usefully compare Butts's Grail novel, *Armed with Madness* (1928), which explicitly seeks this renewal, with the performative and regenerative practices of ritual in John Cowper's *A Glastonbury Romance* (1933). It is unclear whether Butts read any of John Cowper's novels; there is no mention of them in her journals, in which she meticulously listed what she read. However, we know that she read Llewelyn Powys, for she wrote two book reviews of his work, edited and reprinted below, in which she considers two volumes of his gathered prose, *Earth Memories* (1934) and *Dorset Essays* (1935).

Though it appears that Butts did not personally know the Powys brothers, they shared at least one close friend, Louis Wilkinson (1881-1966). Wilkinson stayed with Butts and her second husband, Gabriel Atkin, at their home in Sennen Cove, to the far west of Cornwall, not long after Butts had moved there in 1932, a nervous breakdown in Paris having forced her return to England. Butts's most productive years, in terms of writing, were spent in a small bungalow in Sennen; it is there that she would have written her reviews of Llewelyn's work for the *Sunday Times*. Butts records the visit from Wilkinson in August 1932, when they walked the area and spoke upon topics such as the books of Rebecca West and Aldous Huxley.[1] From Sennen, Wilkinson went on to stay with Llewelyn Powys and Alyse Gregory in Chaldon Herring, from where he wrote a letter to Butts and Atkin, thanking them for their hospitality.[2]

Butts's journals reveal that her opinions of Llewelyn were not confined to her published reviews; an entry for 8 November 1935 describes how her neighbour and close friend, the Scottish translator and art critic Angus Davidson, had joked to her about a Llewelyn 'twined about with tartan shawls' who suffered from a 'distressing "literary diarrhoea"'.[3]

In her two book reviews Butts is kinder to Llewelyn; like many of her articles, they are not always focused on the work being reviewed, but serve for Butts to express her own opinions and to dwell on her favourite topics, and even what we might regard as her obsessions. She believed, as she writes in one of the reviews, that Dorset was the 'county where, if any where, the secret of England is implicit, concealed, yet continuingly giving out the stored forces of its genius.' The 'Neo-pagan' aspects that Butts finds in Llewelyn's work can equally be found in her own brand of natural mysticism that strives to disclose the secrets of England in the Dorset landscape. Butts was just as likely as Llewelyn to 'compare Weymouth Bay with the Lake of Galilee, suggest that the cliffs from Walbarrow Tout west are the shores of Ogygia, where Calypso held Odysseus unwilling, in her arms'.

Dorset (and Wessex) was a sacred landscape for Butts, as it was for the Powys brothers. She shares their respect for its nature and history, knowing that Wessex was, in Butts's withholding phrase, a 'country no man, not Hardy even, has found full words for'.[4] John Cowper had acknowledged Hardy's presence in his preface to *Wood and Stone* (1915), presenting himself and his writing as a nomad lighting a fire in honour of the king — Hardy — whose land he is passing through.[5] John Cowper was mindful that the landscape had already been skilfully mapped, and its places already instilled with contested meanings. In his essays on Dorset, Llewelyn also cannot help but see Hardy in the landscape of which he writes, and feel Hardy shaping his own perceptions and his sensitivities to that landscape; he wonders how often Hardy as a boy had wandered along the river near Lower Bockhampton.[6] Yet while all three writers are aware of Hardy's presence, and that of other lingering myths (along with the sanctity and ferocity of nature itself), each of them is also, for us, a creator of that landscape who shapes our own powers to imagine it. In a journal entry dated 12 March 1922, Butts writes of a visit to a favourite site in Dorset, the Iron Age hill fort of Badbury Rings:

> Enchanted — technically — concretely — if there is such a thing — by reputation, by experience, by tradition. I have felt them — but I have never seen anything but trees & grass & wind & their accompaniments.[7]

Here, the material of nature — trees & grass & wind — exists alongside history and myth, which enchant the place, and give it a life beyond the life of nature. But then Butts explains in her journal: 'We went up the hill to them. I walked first saying *it is I who have given them life*'.[8] She does so through her presence there, through her reading of something historical and mystical in its ruins, and through the words of her own writing. We see a similar meeting of presences in Llewelyn's essays, where nature, mythology and his own practices of walking, reading and writing evoke the Dorset he loved and helped to create. Butts highlights some of these moments in her reviews of those essays.

It might seem strange then that Butts should criticize Llewelyn's descriptions of a '*sacra*' landscape for their 'showmanship'; sacred places are, after all, sites of performance, ritual and display. Though Butts acknowledges Llewelyn to be a good writer, she faults his work as an act of 'display', opening up the countryside to people she deems unwelcome, tourists and the lower classes especially. Butts had addressed this encroachment in a poem of 1932, 'Corfe', whose earlier title is telling: 'A Song to Keep People out of Dorset'. Butts also finds fault with Llewelyn's 'neo-paganism', suggesting that a lack of 'faith' and denial of the 'Grace of God' will not allow him to 'penetrate into the inner meaning of a land … whose history and faith [he] believe[s] to be founded on error.' Butts is alluding to the role that Christianity — Roman Catholicism in particular — has played in the South West. With a keen interest in Dorset history, and as an advocate for the continued influence of older landed families as paternalistic landlords, Butts would have known of the Weld family, one of the great Catholic families of England, and landowners of a large swathe of the coast of southeast Dorset around Lulworth; the Weld Estate was the landlord for all the Powyses living in Chaldon Herring and Chydyok. Butts's revived Catholic faith would motivate this criticism of Llewelyn. Yet her disapproval is amusing when we consider the paganism that informs Butts's own writing — she even studied under the occultist Aleister Crowley in 1921 — and continues significantly to colour her own eclectic version of Catholicism.

In her reviews we find a muted praise and some criticism of Llewelyn's view of Dorset, and in them we also see the view preferred by Mary Butts, the connections she makes, the powers she invokes, and the landscape that she (also) adored. While highlighting the practices that shape and create the Dorset landscape in Llewelyn's work, her articles become part of those same practices, in the ongoing creation of a land sacred and beloved.

'Mr Powys's Dorset', the *Sunday Times*, 18 February 1934, p. 11
Review of *Earth Memories*, by Llewelyn Powys

These are Neo-pagan essays, distinguished from many by a real spontaneous delight in all that is implied by 'being out of doors'. The book exhibits the attitude of our age, uncertain of any good and agonisingly conscious of only too much that is wrong; sure of one good only, that the works of nature are exquisite, diverse, glorious, and free to all. The greater part is made up of studies of Dorset, the county where, if any where, the secret of England is implicit, concealed, yet continuingly giving out the stored forces of its genius.

Passing over an excursion on Peter Breughel the Elder, and a rather gratuitous attack on the Merton dons for not being in sympathy with something that is outside their function, there is one essay, 'The Blind Cow', that gives the essence of the book: 'The Blind Cow', the blunt rock the sea rolls over, near where the author found a guillemot, its pure breast clogged with oil, filthy and piteously condemned to death. Before he saw that, he had even begun to hope that the bright fish threading the waters round the Blind Cow, the 'exultation' of larks above it in the air, *might* be 'signatures for certain whispers of hope, challenging to the selfish, absolute domination of the Blind Cow.' A hope reconsidered when the guillemot died, 'perhaps from fright, perhaps from despair'.

One of the countless deaths it would cost man nothing to make impossible. Will he wait till there is an indestructible scum over the face of the whole sea?

In the Name of Truth

This essay, and it is exceedingly well and even beautifully written, gives the temper of the book: its philosophy is essentially that of Mr. Huxley's — that God is nothing more than a name for a series of man-made assumptions and hypotheses. While for alternative, the somehow rather strident, rather metallic cult of belief in the number of alternative daemonic powers interior and exterior to man is all we are offered.

All in the name of intellectual honesty. The terrible difficulty is — why cannot intellectual honesty, the old-fashioned love of truth, find something more satisfying! A little more daring is perhaps indicated; a little more genius. But the last cannot be had to order. The Grace of God is what is wanted. Only that, it appears, by some necessity inherent in itself, cannot be given without faith. And faith, as Lytton Strachey pointed out, speaking of official circles in 1870, is no longer considered necessary to the knowledge of God.

Again, it would seem that humility enters in. As Miss Batho, in her recent book on Wordsworth, pointed out, if Wordsworth was right, 'Mr. Huxley is making himself unnecessarily miserable'. To Wordsworth's what a catalogue of great names can be added! Perhaps at this stage the only answer is that *attendu le sens commun*; the world has found a fuller life by listening to such men as Wordsworth than by even the strictest attention to Mr. Huxley and Mr. Powys.

'Dorset Essays: Scenes and Memories', the *Sunday Times*, 24 November 1935, p. 16
Review of *Dorset Essays*, by Llewelyn Powys

It is becoming a more and more undeniable fact that some counties are news. Gone is the blessed ignorance that endured at least until a century ago when a family in Herefordshire was as likely to visit Devon as it was to visit the moon.

Now, for better or worse — and the worse is becoming daily more obvious — every inch of these islands is becoming almost instantly accessible to anyone with a little time on his hands and a share of the townsman's morbid curiosity about rural life. By which he means, in essence, the picturesque. Which is everything he has no business to mean. Now, as again was inevitable, we are urged to become 'country-conscious' in a way which might distress Mr. Llewelyn Powys as much as it would have distressed Thomas Hardy.

This is not to attack Mr. Llewelyn Powys. There is a great demand for such books. Writers must live. He has really lived in Dorset; and it is something to be spared the slush of the essential non-resident, out to patronise, to be amused, to be thrilled, or to escape. Out indeed — sometimes with the best intentions — to parade the distorted values which are the appalling legacy of our urbanised, popular-science-ridden world.

Indeed, these essays appear as an ardent homage to the writer's native land. They range all over the county, from the Fossil Forest at Lulworth, life on the mysterious headland, the White Nose, Studland, and the Great Heath to the green wood mounting above Crichel. They are most beautifully illustrated, and dedicated with all appearance of piety to 'our two fathers', rectors of Montacute since 1845.[9] Also the author's wide reading picks up old memories; he is at home with ancient traditions; he can compare Weymouth Bay with the Lake of Galilee, suggest that the cliffs from Walbarrow Tout west are the shores of Ogygia, where Calypso held Odysseus unwilling, in her arms.

Almost one feels that this book would pass for a paean on a part of our land that its 'sons and lovers' feel to be more sacred, more 'numinous' than any other place. Because of this, because such *sacra* were not meant for display, one can only call it a work of showmanship.

It goes without saying that this book is of far higher quality than most of the rhapsodies and the familiarities we have had to endure. But how can such writers penetrate into the inner meaning of a land the whole pattern of whose history and faith they believe to be founded on error?

NOTES

[1] Mary Butts, Journal entries dated 16 and 20 August 1932, in *The Journals of Mary Butts*, ed. Nathalie Blondel (New Haven: Yale University Press, 2002), 396; see also Nathalie Blondel, *Mary Butts: Scenes from the Life* (New York: McPherson, 1998), 307.
[2] See Blondel, *Mary Butts: Scenes from the Life*, 307.
[3] Journal entry dated 8 November 1935, in *The Journals of Mary Butts*, 451.
[4] Mary Butts, *The Crystal Cabinet: my childhood at Salterns*, 2nd edn (Boston: Beacon-Press, 1988), 63.
[5] John Cowper Powys, *Wood and Stone: A Romance* (New York: G. Arnold Shaw, 1915), xi.
[6] Llewelyn Powys, *Dorset Essays* (London: John Lane The Bodley Head, 1935), 184.
[7] Journal entry dated 12 March 1922, in *The Journals of Mary Butts*, 194.
[8] Journal entry cited by Blondel in *Mary Butts: Scenes from the Life*, 114.
[9] By 'our fathers' Llewelyn includes Wyndham Goodden whose photographs accompany Llewelyn's essays: Charles Francis Powys had succeeded Goodden's father as the incumbent of Montacute.

JEREMY HOOKER

From 'God's Houses'

St Peter and St Paul, Mappowder

With thoughts of T.F. Powys

1

Muck on country lanes,
good dirt,
and fields of Blackmore Vale
and distant Bulbarrow.

A place where a man
might hide himself from the world.

This, however, was a man
on no map known to us
though he chose to live here,
close to the churchyard wall
communing with the dead.

His tomb is a stone book,
the last enigmatic page
given over to the grass.

2

Obliteration
was his word for death,
a final consignment
of all he was to silence,
a gift to God's Acre.

There is, perhaps, a mystery of the self
that reaches beyond the self,
a silence that deepens
beyond the word.

3

I have sat where he sat
in a pew of the empty church
listening, wondering
about this man.

I have followed his steps
on the Dorset lane,
smelling the good smell
of sun-warmed dirt,
watching skylark and peewit
over fields towards Bulbarrow,
entranced by tiny things,
grass seed and celandine,
ditches humming with summer.

I have read his words
and thought at times
I glimpsed a mind I might know.

But each time he escaped
as perhaps he too, listening
for the dead beyond the wall
escaped from himself, reaching
into depths he could not fathom.

Under the Shadow of the Oath: A Selection from the African Journals of Mary Casey

Edited and introduced by LOUISE DE BRUIN

Kijabe, Kenya: Old Africa Books, 2012. 216 pp. ISBN: 978-9966-757-02-9. £9.99.

Anyone familiar with Mary Casey's writings but previously unaware of the facts of her life in Africa is likely to be surprised, as I was, by aspects of this publication. In these pages one hears of the poet learning to fire a rifle, and taking a revolver with her on a walk in the forest. It is in some ways a desperate story the journals have to tell. For Gerard and Mary Casey were farming in Kenya during the period of the Mau Mau Emergency, when sheep and cattle were slashed and killed, farms burned, and near neighbours, Europeans and Africans, murdered.

Horror and acts of cruelty are graphically described in these pages, which cover the period from August 1950 until the end of 1957. As Louise de Bruin explains in her informative Introduction, the title 'refers to the oaths taken by those of the Kikuyu revolting against the colonial powers; a rebellion that became known as the Mau Mau Uprising or State of Emergency'. The Caseys evidently treated the Africans working for them well, but with men among them 'who have taken blood-curdling oaths for your destruction', their lives are in constant danger, and their work — eventually they farmed some 5,000 sheep and 2,000 head of cattle — goes on under the shadow.

We learn that the Caseys supported Col David Stirling's Capricorn Africa Society which opposed racial discrimination. Mary was pointedly critical of some fellow Europeans. When attending a settlers' meeting she is disturbed by the 'self-righteousness', and remarks: 'There was no hint that anything might be said for the other side, for the people in whose land we make our living, no attempt to admit our own shortcomings; or to confess our own words and actions towards these people were in some measure the cause of the present evil plight'.

The story is by no means all horror. Mary Casey was acutely sensitive to the beauty of Africa, and, like all Powyses, she loved the elements. The journals consequently contain marvellous descriptions of Kenyan landscapes and wild creatures, especially birds, and of weathers and night skies, as well as harrowing accounts of drought and flood. But when she encountered horror she looked at it unflinchingly. This looking, at horror and beauty alike, is a distinguishing feature of the journals. She observes a 'striking bird with bright chestnut feathers and white head that runs on spidery toes upon the lily leaves'. She looks with the same clarity of vision at a scene of killed sheep: 'A last sun ray darted into a disembowelled wether and the inside of his ribs showed a most vividly gleaming scarlet lining. ... The pile of lustrous bellies and guts grows bigger. The men pause, wipe their gory fingers in the grass and take snuff. Hens with gay combs come about inquisitively, pecking at the blood clots'. The journals are rich in appreciation of both wild creatures and sheep and cattle, but completely without sentimentality. Leopards and lions and rhinos, as well as wild dogs, which are a danger to the herds, have to be hunted down and killed.

Gerard more than once remarked to me on Powys toughness. It is abundantly evident here, in Will Powys, Mary's uncle and godfather, who farms within visiting distance of the Caseys, and in Mary herself. There are clearly times when she misses her mother and English country, and thinks longingly of her original home at Horsebridge Mill in Hampshire; for some months she is hospitalized with tuberculosis, but she is entirely without self-pity, whether for her medical state or for the emotional turbulence to which she is prone. Her control in face of inner and outer conflict is what makes her seeing so fearless.

Practical and dedicated farmers, Mary and Gerard Casey are also students. Mary translates a poem of Heine's and passages from Homer; Gerard learns Sanskrit; he reads René Guenon and they talk about 'the lost art of contemplation'. Mary values her Christian heritage, but in this period her attitude to life is stoic and profoundly Homeric. For her, Homer's two great epics 'echo the high triumph of man — music, poetry, defiance of fate and resignation to fate when all is lost'.

Mary Casey had written poems before, and she wrote a few poems — though very few — during this particular time in Africa. The great 'release' of her poetry was to occur in the following decade, stimulated by her romantic friendship with Valentine Ackland and influenced by her discovery of the philosophy of Plotinus, which enhanced her understanding of 'aloneness'. Her main writing during this period in Africa was her novel (she calls it 'story'), still unpublished, *Egbert of England*, and above all the journal itself. It is nevertheless, a poet's journal, as revealed in both its reflections on poetic language and its style. The following passage is especially significant in this respect:

> Yes, I am sure it was Shelley who first enchanted my ear with the magic of words, who taught me how every word has its own singular and private poetry which it repeats silently to itself until the one who makes use of it releases this inward music by assigning the word to its exact position in his stanzas. It was very likely from the Greeks that he caught this heaven-sent art.

Here, even as she speaks of the importance of positioning words she is placing her own words with poetic care for meaning and rhythm. 'Magic of words' and 'inward music' are not separate from linguistic discipline. Romantic poetic practice has its roots in ancient poetry.

In a later entry Mary Casey writes: 'What I love best is an image, a reflection of nature in the mind that is not uninfluenced by thought, however sad or gay; winging or stagnant the thought may be, but it is the meaning of sky and forest and plain, swift deer and what engenders fear'. This is the essential process of Mary Casey's poetry: nature in the mind, and the thinking, feeling mind in nature. It is how her imagination worked, and in consequence many passages in the journals have the quality of prose poetry. For example:

> At tea-time the sky grew stormy. A vulture glided so slowly across the new greyness that covered part of the sky it seemed without motion. Then came all the rare delights of splendid fleeting sunlight, silver raindrops, the dead cedars like white-frozen fire. The dark hush when the sunlight fled. We stayed by the waterfall hearing the plash, waiting upon the overlaying forms of fern fronds, the long and delicate trailing stems of creepers with heart-shaped leaves, softly green as in England.

The first entry in this selection, 13 August 1950, simply records 'Llewelyn's birthday'. The dramatic, colourful cover reproduces one of Will Powys's paintings of Mount Kenya. Will is a noble presence in these pages. Mary's mind often turns to other members of the family as well: to the influence on her of JCP's philosophy, and to her mother and Gertrude in particular. In herself and through other Powyses she feels the depth of family history:

> Oh, but it was good to see Will, he sat for a while on the veranda enjoying the quiet and the evening sky. 'My mother was always fond of the dusk', he said, pronouncing the last word with a particular intonation so that I seemed to feel the quality of some long summer twilight at Montacute.

Mary Casey experiences the ultimate aloneness that is, paradoxically, a characteristic Powyses share. At one time she says: 'Any way as John teaches, preaches and repeats over and over again every single, human being is completely alone and can only find happiness by recognizing it, and learning to find his most priceless enjoyment of life in this very inescapable and thrilling solitude'. Reading this, we may reflect that if the young Gerard Casey had not discovered a copy of *Philosophy of Solitude* in Bridgend Public Library he and Mary would never have met.

Mary Casey's inner strength, which is plain to see on every page of this selection from her African journals, is of an heroic quality. It is one she shares with Will and with Gerard. Gerard's presence in the journals is all the more remarkable for being undemonstrative. He supports Mary in every way, and goes about his demanding and often dangerous work with quiet courage, perhaps having to venture out after dark to set a trap for a lion, yet finding time to read with Mary, to translate Virgil, and to learn Sanskrit. His and Mary's lives in Kenya are indeed Homeric. For our knowledge of their experience we are indebted once again, as for her work on the first published selection of Mary Casey's journals, *A Net in Water*, to Louise de Bruin. Her loyal and painstaking editorial labour has a heroism of its own.

Jeremy Hooker

Mary Casey on the Beale farm in 1952

Women's Writing: The Ways and Wiles of Obscurity

CHARLES LOCK

Patterns on the Sand
GAMEL WOOLSEY, with an Introduction by Barbara Ozieblo
Sherborne: Sundial Press, 2012. ISBN 978-1-908274-13-7 £16.99.

A Cage for the Nightingale
PHYLLIS PAUL, with an Introduction by Glen Cavaliero
Sherborne: Sundial Press, 2012. ISBN 978-1-908274-11-3 £16.50.

With the Hunted: Selected Writings
SYLVIA TOWNSEND WARNER, edited by Peter Tolhurst
Norwich: Black Dog Books, 2012. ISBN 978-0-9565672-3-9 £14.50.

The Sundial Press continues its invaluable work of bringing out or back books from the periphery of 'the Powys Circle'; its authors include Alyse Gregory, Elizabeth Myers, David Garnett, Littleton Powys, Philippa Powys and now Gamel Woolsey. One circle's periphery is another circle's centre; one point can be on quite distinct peripheries; such a publishing venture as Sundial's can help us to see through circle, gnomon and shadow the linkings and overlappings of literary history, as well as offering some exceptionally good reading.

Gamel Woolsey died in 1968; she was born in 1897 (or thereabouts) and was raised prosperously in South Carolina; her aunt Sarah Chauncey Woolsey is known under her pen-name Susan Coolidge as the author of *What Katy Did* (1872); her half-brother John M. Woolsey is universally honoured for his judicial ruling in 1933 that allowed the sale and distribution in the United States of James Joyce's *Ulysses*. Her second novel, *Patterns on the Sand*, seems to have been written in the years before 1947 when it was submitted for publication and rejected. The manuscript was identified only in 2000, by Barbara Ozieblo who provides a most informative introduction. (Ozieblo's essay 'The Poet Gamel Woolsey' in *PJ* XIII is invaluable, and a foretaste of her forthcoming dual biography of Gamel Woolsey and Alyse Gegory.) In 1922 Gamel moved to New York where she lived with her half-brother John in 5 Patchin Place; thus in due time she came to know the occupants of no. 4. Her relationship with Llewelyn Powys is well documented — not least by decoding his novel *Love and Death* - and its significance has been drawn out with care and sensitivity, elsewhere in the present volume, by Arjen Mulder.

Kenneth Hopkins was a pioneering advocate for Gamel Woolsey in the 1970s, and is responsible for having brought much of her poetry into print. Virago issued what ought to have been Gamel's first novel, *One Way of Love*, in 1987; the work had been set up in type in 1932 before the publisher, fearing the law, withdrew it. That publisher was Victor Gollancz, the very same who — twenty-five years later — deleted one risky word in James Purdy's *63: Dream Palace* to incur the displeasure of Edith Sitwell and John Cowper Powys. Frances Partridge, whose husband Ralph had been a close friend of Gamel's husband Gerald Brenan, is our best witness to the non-appearance of *One Way of Love*:

> It was unfortunately withdrawn on the verge of publication in 1932 because the publishers' nerve had been shaken by the prosecution of Radclyffe Hall's *The Well of Loneliness* for lesbianism not long before. This must have been a maddeningly frustrating event for Gamel, who accepted it with almost saintly mildness, as I well remember. (*Death's Other Kingdom*, Virago 1988, vii)

A book banned in one country but available in others — such as *Ulysses*, or *Spycatcher* — is likely to become a focus of protest and controversy, and subsequently of historical interest; but a book not published anywhere might leave no trace at all beyond the immediate circle of its author: it is possible that Gamel's frustration over *One Way of Love* in 1932 influenced the judicial thinking of her half-brother the following year. It is worth noting, however, that Gamel told Llewelyn that she had never known John Woolsey well, though 'I am delighted with him for being so courageous and fair-minded over Ulysses.' (K. Hopkins, *Letters of Gamel Woolsey to Llewelyn Powys 1930-39*, Warren House: 1983, 58)

In 1939 Longman published Gamel's memoir of the Spanish Civil War, *Death's Other Kingdom*, with a preface by John Cowper Powys. When this was re-issued by Virago in 1988, John Cowper's preface was dropped and its place taken by Frances Partridge. Thus we see Gamel moved from the periphery of one circle to that of another; she figures regularly in Frances Partridge's *Diaries*, though seldom vividly; she's there, of course, in Ralph Partridge's correspondence with Brenan, *Best of Friends* (ed. Xan Fielding, Cape, 1986), but never quite present.

Those already familiar with *One Way of Love* and *Death's Other Kingdom* will hardly need persuading of Gamel's literary art. It involves a cultivated appearance of artlessness mingled with learned allusiveness, and can switch from the reassuring to the disconcerting. On first reading *Patterns on the Sand* one might assume that it was written before *One Way of Love*; its setting is the South Carolina of Gamel's youth, and the novel has the feel of an early work. (It must be said that this novel draws on Gamel's life before she went to New York, so it has none of the evocations of Patchin Place, even mentions of Powyses, that make *One Way of Love* a work of documentary value for Powysians.) *Patterns on the Sand* may seem simple enough, but a sense of the predictable and straightforward ought to give way to an appreciation of something else at work. The novel's final paragraph may be cited here (it discloses nothing of the plot):

> On every side of them, in that sea-beleaguered region, the great outsetting movement had begun. From all the creeks and inlets which the tide had filled the salt water came welling and streaming back.

Yet much of the book if of a tone as banal and almost as startling as this passage in *One Way of Love*:

> They stopped at a fried fish shop in the King's Road, for the restaurants were all closed for Boxing Day, and bought two sixpenny pieces of fish. This price includes a quantity of potato chips and vinegar if you wish it.

The shift in tense is disconcerting, and the direct address to the reader jolts us, for it says not only: would you like to join us? but also: are you paying attention? This is characteristic of Woolsey's art, that stays on the periphery yet looks as though it delights to be found out. The more one reads by Gamel, and about her, the more readily we can take the measure of John Cowper telling James Purdy: 'I think Gamel is Phyllis's best friend.'

Phyllis Playter, that is, rather than Phyllis Paul, whom both John Cowper and his Phyllis so admired. To James Purdy they recommended three titles: *Camila* (*sic*), *The Lion of Cooling Bay* and *Rox Hall Illuminated*, especially the latter. These were published in respectively 1949, 1953 and 1956. Nothing of hers has been in print for fifty years, so the re-issuing of *A Cage for the Nightingale* is an event, at least for the few, the very few, who know her name at all. Unlike Gamel who frequents peripheries and is easily tracked through the diaries and memoirs of others, Phyllis Paul lived alone and left almost no trace. Glen Cavaliero tells us in the foreword that when in 1973, aged 70, she was run over by a motorcyclist, 'she was only identified by a label on her pocket handkerchief'.

Virtually nothing is known of her. Yet there can be doubt that she is a most peculiar novelist. I used the word not in disdain but to emphasize how different this novel is from anything else. It is not experimental in any of the obvious senses; rather it conceals itself behind the stage props of a murder mystery of the age of Dorothy L. Sayers or (Paul's exact contemporary) Margery Allingham. The mystery is that the murder is not solved, and the reader begins to wonder whether it's an exercise in pastiche, whether everybody has conspired together to commit the murder (as on the Orient Express), or whether the murderer is whoever thinks that he or she has done it.

Like John Cowper's novels, this one has no protagonist, nor any person on whom the reader can rely: whoever we might take to be a constant imparter of information and reflection will abandon that role. Insofar as anything might be characteristic, we could consider this:

> Back in her own room, she took a long, hypnotized look at herself in the glass. 'What is going on?' she thought. The double, as such doubles do, seemed to be full of dark knowledge which it would not impart.

The double, as such doubles do: it is not enough to introduce the uncanny, the *Unheimlich*, it must be mentioned as though we were all familiar with it, were even indeed its familiars. It is little wonder that among Phyllis Paul's admirers was Elizabeth Bowen. Just as our reliable characters seem to be less than wholly so, so those against whom we have our suspicions are found to be themselves suspecting. Much here depends on the power of suggestion, and especially of suggestion voiced by authority: or by authority being established by the quality of suggestion, both articulated and withheld. It is as though we do not know what we have seen or what we have heard until we are told, are offered a version to which we can give our assent. Thus when we believe that we have been witnesses to an event, we might be merely passing on somebody else's narrative. Every witness is thus implicated in the case, and among the guilty must be all who have spoken.

This gives a far from adequate sense of *A Cage for the Nightingale*; the book does defy description and classification. We might hazard that it has the manner and structure of a short story: one expects to be able to keep up the uncertainties and the enigmas for twenty pages or so. Yet it goes on for 250 pages; we live with the setting as though it were a novel, but with the characters as though they were passing by. Of course any mystery demands that we cannot be permitted to know the characters well, and their thoughts are seldom offered. There is thus a controlled supply of inwardness in the persons, yet a novelistic depth in the setting. This is not quite the generic vicarage and village of the detective novel. The large house to the side of the village is reminiscent of Emily Brontë or Hardy, or of John Cowper, and the reader has no trouble adjusting to the scenery or learning the topography, the layout of the corridors, the village and its roads. The characters, by contrast, are not so easily mapped; they frustrate us, and it is that frustration that is for the patient reader transformed into enigma.

No publisher need be given credit for drawing our attention to a neglected figure when the writer in question is Sylvia Townsend Warner. *With the Hunted* is subtitled 'Selected Writings' which is quite misleading, for there is none of her fiction here, nor of her letters and diaries. I had put it to one side, thinking it to be merely an anthology. In fact it contains her essays, reviews and other forms of non-fictional writing, often reprinted for the first time since their initial appearance in *The Countryman*, *Britain Today* and similarly recondite journals. A 'proper publisher' would know how to promote this volume as the collected essays of one of the great writers of the twentieth century. But Black Dog Books knows nothing of such vulgar hype; it describes itself as 'an independent publisher specialising in East Anglian literature and the arts' which is entirely admirable but hardly the imprint for such an important volume as this. *With the Hunted* is one of just five volumes on the publisher's list. This sounds ungrateful, and one is of course extremely grateful to have these essays made available. But indignation needs to be registered; there is nothing controversial in the editor Peter Tolhurst, comparing Sylvia Townsend Warner to Virginia Woolf. Her critical standing is high and her ranking in terms of political correctness is almost embarrassing: leftist, feminist and lesbian.

The paradox of this publication is made clear by the space accorded it in the *TLS*: *With the Hunted* was the subject of the main review, by Claire Harman, Warner's biographer, in the issue dated 5 October 2012. Harmon dwells at some length on the problem of Warner's reputation. If one of Warner's were an essay by Woolf, Harman writes, it 'would have been collected, reprinted and edited several times … would be available in all its variant forms, exhaustively footnoted and commented on.' Harman speaks of 'Warner's obscurity' and of course laments this state of things. And yet the utterance belied the grievance: not only was this book from a very small press given the main review in the *TLS*, but a delightful David Levine-style cartoon of Sylvia lit up that week's cover. And every word of Sylvia's within this volume can light up the moment. Her British Council pamphlet on Jane Austen is reprinted in its twenty pithy pages; of all that has been written about Jane Austen since 1951, one might ask how much of it was necessary.

In an essay of considerable force and foresight, 'Women as Writers', delivered as a lecture to the Royal Society of Arts in 1959, Warner makes an unwelcome point about women writers, that they are almost all of the middle class, and the few exceptions are not of the working class:

> Apart from one or two grandees like Mme de La Fayette, women writers have come from the middle class, and their writing carries a heritage of middle-class virtues; good taste, prudence, acceptance of limitations, compliance with standards, and that typically middle-class merit of making the most of what one's got....

And this means that there are no women writing from the conditions of living and observing that give us the work of Clare or Burns or Bunyan. (Warner writes extremely well on Defoe and Richardson.) On the larger problem of women in literature, Warner subordinates the question of gender to class analysis:

> So when we consider women as writers, we must bear in mind that we have not very much to go on, and that it is too early to assess what they may be capable of. It may well be that the half has not yet been told us: that unbridled masterpieces, daring innovations, epics, tragedies, works of genial impropriety — all the things that women have so far signally failed to produce — have been socially, not sexually, debarred; that at this moment a Joan Milton or a Françoise Rabelais may have left the washing unironed and the stew uncared for because she can't wait to begin.

One might dare to ask whether the class origin of women writers in Britain has changed much, if at all, in the past fifty years; and why Warner's essay is not read wherever they read 'A Room of One's Own'.

Warner's obscurity is hardly to be matched against Phyllis Paul's, though it may be compared with that of other women writers of critically acclaimed distinction; one thinks of Dorothy M. Richardson. This may not be a problem peculiar to women writers. Those of us who have thought John Cowper worth keeping in print may think that scant regard need be accorded to gender. Sylvia's friend T. F. Powys — all of whose scattered writings on whom are gathered in *With the Hunted* — might be today in similar case, though forty years ago he seemed firmly affixed, albeit in a minor canon, and much more so than John Cowper. Obscurity and its ways, and ways out therefrom, have troubled my thoughts in reading these books, each enjoyed, and (regarding Phyllis Paul and Gamel Woolsey) with a sense of the good fortune that should have brought such books my way: this is feasting on the Powys periphery. And wondering at the vagaries of textual fortunes: how much obscurity must a writer suffer, and of how long durance, before some kind publisher takes up the cause? *With the Hunted* I have read — as I'd hope to read anything of Sylvia's — in a condition of textual euphoria akin to that induced by Jane Austen; yet on this occasion a delight spiced with indignation that this volume should be mine merely by luck, not in consequence of universal admiration. If this can fall into obscurity, what's to be spared? The Sundial Press is well named, for a sundial can be a reliable indicator, but it is of no use under a cloud.

ADVISORY BOARD

Robert Caserio — Penn State University, USA
Glen Cavaliero — St Catharine's College, Cambridge, UK
H.W. Fawkner — Stockholm University, Sweden
Peter J. Foss — UK
David Goodway — University of Leeds, UK
Jeremy Hooker — University of Glamorgan, UK
W.J. Keith — University of Toronto, Canada
Morine Krisdóttir — UK
J. Lawrence Mitchell — Texas A & M University, USA
Elmar Schenkel — Leipzig University, Germany
John Williams — University of Greenwich, London, UK

NOTES ON CONTRIBUTORS

MICHAEL BALLIN, Emeritus Professor of English, Wilfrid Laurier University, Ontario, continues to work on John Cowper Powys and literary modernism.

JONATHAN GOODWIN is an Assistant Professor of English at the University of Louisiana at Lafayette. He has essays published or forthcoming on James Joyce, Wyndham Lewis and John le Carré; his essay on *A Glastonbury Romance* is in Volume XVII of the *Powys Journal*.

JOEL HAWKES is revising for publication the doctoral thesis that he defended at the University of Bristol in 2011: a study of linguistic representations and ritual practices of the Wessex landscape. He currently teaches at Thompson Rivers University in British Columbia.

JEREMY HOOKER, Emeritus Professor at the University of South Wales, is a poet and essayist; he has recently been elected a Fellow of the Learned Society of Wales. The *Cut of the Light: Poems 1965-2005* (Enitharmon) is a substantial selection from his ten published volumes. A new collection of poems is forthcoming, as is a study of modern poetry and British landscape painting. *Openings: A European Journal* — a sequel to *Welsh Journal* (2002) and *Upstate: A North American Journal* (2007) — is due from Shearsman later this year.

CHARLES LOCK is Professor of English Literature at the University of Copenhagen; in 2011 he was appointed Knight of the Order of the Dannebrog. Recent publications include essays on Rose Macaulay, Helen Waddell, Patrick White and Geoffrey Hill.

ARJEN MULDER is an essayist and biologist. Based in Amsterdam, he teaches at art schools in Holland and Belgium. He has published a number of books, some of which are translated into English: *Book for the Electronic Arts* (2000), *Understanding Media Theory* (2004), and *From Image to Interaction* (2010). Not yet translated are his study, *The Woman for whom Cesare Pavese Committed Suicide* (2005), and a novel *The Third Boy* (2004).